AMERICAN ★ HISTORY

The PROGRESSIVE ERA

Activists Change America

By David Anthony

Portions of this book originally appeared in
The Progressive Era by Kevin Hillstrom.

LUCENT PRESS

Published in 2018 by
Lucent Press, an Imprint of Greenhaven Publishing, LLC
353 3rd Avenue
Suite 255
New York, NY 10010

Designer: Deanna Paternostro
Editor: Siyavush Saidian

Cataloging-in-Publication Data

Names: Anthony, David.
Title: The progressive era: activists change America / David Anthony.
Description: New York : Lucent Press, 2018. | Series: American history | Includes index.
Identifiers: ISBN 9781534561397 (library bound) | ISBN 9781534561403 (ebook)
Subjects: LCSH: Social action–Juvenile literature. | Social change–Juvenile literature.
Classification: LCC HN18.3 A58 2018 | DDC 361.3'7–dc23

Printed in the United States of America

CPSIA compliance information: Batch #BS17KL: For further information contact Greenhaven Publishing LLC, New York, New York at 1-844-317-7404.

Please visit our website, www.greenhavenpublishing.com. For a free color catalog of all our high-quality books, call toll free 1-844-317-7404 or fax 1-844-317-7405.

Contents

Foreword   4

Setting the Scene: A Timeline   6

Introduction:
    From Industry to Progress   8

Chapter One:
    Increasing Industrialism   12

Chapter Two:
    Society and Politics   30

Chapter Three:
    Big Business and Little Labor   48

Chapter Four:
    Presidential Policies   64

Epilogue:
    No End to Progress   78

Notes   92

For More Information   95

Index   97

Picture Credits   103

About the Author   104

Foreword

The United States is a relatively young country. It has existed as its own nation for more than 200 years, but compared to nations such as China that have existed since ancient times, it is still in its infancy. However, the United States has grown and accomplished much since its birth in 1776. What started as a loose confederation of former British colonies has grown into a major world power whose influence is felt around the globe.

How did the United States manage to develop into a global superpower in such a short time? The answer lies in a close study of its unique history. The story of America is unlike any other—filled with colorful characters, a variety of exciting settings, and events too incredible to be anything other than true.

Too often, the experience of history is lost among the basic facts: names, dates, places, laws, treaties, and battles. These fill countless textbooks, but they are rarely compelling on their own. Far more interesting are the stories that surround those

basic facts. It is in discovering those stories that students are able to see history as a subject filled with life—and a subject that says as much about the present as it does about the past.

The titles in this series allow readers to immerse themselves in the action at pivotal historical moments. They also encourage readers to discuss complex issues in American history—many of which still affect Americans today. These include racism, states' rights, civil liberties, and many other topics that are in the news today but have their roots in the earliest days of America. As such, readers are encouraged to think critically about history and current events.

Each title is filled with excellent tools for research and analysis. Fully cited quotations from historical figures, letters, speeches, and documents provide students with firsthand accounts of major events. Primary sources bring authority to the text, as well. Sidebars highlight these quotes and primary sources, as well as interesting figures and events. Annotated bibliographies allow students to locate and evaluate sources for further information on the subject.

A deep understanding of America's past is necessary to understand its present and its future. Sometimes you have to look back to see how to best move forward, and that is certainly true when writing the next chapter in the American story.

1890

Jacob Riis publishes *How the Other Half Lives: Studies among the Tenements of New York*, exposing the horrible social conditions of poor New Yorkers; the Sherman Antitrust Act is passed but has little power.

1899

One of the first Progressive activist groups, the National Consumers' League, is founded to fight for fairer working conditions.

1890	1893	1899	1901–1902

1893

Supporting the Prohibitionist cause, the Anti-Saloon League is formed and campaigns to outlaw alcohol in America.

1901–1902

Theodore Roosevelt becomes president of the United States; the United Mine Workers of America union calls for the largest strike in U.S. history; President Roosevelt successfully dissolves the Northern Securities Company.

A Timeline

1904–1906

President Roosevelt institutes his Square Deal policy, focusing on breaking up large trusts and conserving America's wildlife; Upton Sinclair, labeled a muckraker, publishes *The Jungle*, a book about labor abuses; the Hepburn Act is passed, which gives the Interstate Commerce Commission more power.

1917

The United States is drawn into World War I after German ships attack merchant vessels; the Russian Revolution takes place, removing Czar Nicholas II from the throne.

| 1904–1906 | 1909–1911 | 1917 | 1918–1920 |

1909–1911

Influential African American activists establish the National Association for the Advancement of Colored People (NAACP); nearly 150 workers die in the Triangle Shirtwaist Factory fire.

1918–1920

The United States emerges victorious from World War I with a powerful economy and army; support for the Progressive movement dramatically declines; fear of Communism leads to the Red Scare, which is used by American corporations to discredit labor strikes.

FROM INDUSTRY TO PROGRESS

Beginning in the 18th century in England and eventually spreading to the United States and other parts of the world over the next century, the Industrial Revolution is among the most important events in world history. A number of new machines, including the steam engine, were invented and refined during the Industrial Revolution. New strategies for the workforce were introduced, such as the assembly line and factory models of manufacturing. In 19th-century America, the most noticeable immediate effects were in the fields of industry and production. Manufacturers now had the ability to use higher quality materials, such as steel, and the new labor models helped factories increase their productivity to unprecedented highs. In turn, this brought massive profits to large business owners and powerful corporations.

As industry and production were flourishing, however, the common people were suffering. Businesses generated fortunes, but little of the increased wealth was distributed among the workers. Most unskilled laborers were forced to work in unsafe and difficult conditions, typically in large factories where they were employed to do repetitive and mindless tasks for long hours every day. Furthermore, because wages were so low, some families could not afford to support themselves unless they brought their children to work as well. The first federal laws against child labor were not passed in the United States until 1916. As millions of working-class Americans watched their corporate bosses get richer, they also saw themselves getting poorer. This introduced feelings of anger and bitterness in the working class. These were the first whisperings of a class conflict that has persisted for centuries.

A New Movement

Millions of working-class and middle-class Americans felt that they were powerless to stand against the railroad magnates, bankers, and manufacturing tycoons who controlled the nation's political and industrial arenas. As the century drew to a close, "the United States was not one nation, but several; it was a land divided by region, race, and ethnicity. And it was a land still deeply split by class conflict … wage workers, farmers, and the rich were alien to one another."[1] The business leaders in the middle and latter years of the 19th century were so powerful, in fact, that many people believed that they were taking over the government. For millions of Americans, this was completely unacceptable; the democratic process was the foundation of the United States, and people were not going to willingly allow big corporations to take control of it.

After decades of rising anger and resentment, the turn of the 20th century was also a turning point in American history. Though industry was still explosively successful, common people were increasingly discontented. In response to these troubling times, a popular movement, known as Progressivism, swept across the nation in the first two decades of the 1900s. This movement was driven by a number of different groups, each of which had a unique set of priorities. Some were dedicated to addressing the crushing poverty and terrible working conditions that afflicted industrial America. Others set their sights on fixing the nation's problems of political corruption and gender discrimination.

The leadership of the Progressive

Jane Addams established a settlement house in Chicago, Illinois, where the poor could go for food, shelter, and educational classes.

Mary Harris "Mother" Jones was an influential and controversial Progressive leader. She was a cofounder of the Industrial Workers of the World, a Socialist union.

goal: reforming and improving American society for the benefit of everyone.

The activists and supporters of reform during America's Progressive Era shared a similar view of the American government and its appropriate role in the lives of its citizens. They believed that the economic and social forces unleashed by the Industrial Revolution required the government to take a more active role in managing the nation's fortunes and economy than it had ever done before. Unlike earlier generations of Americans who had been suspicious of government regulation, especially in the marketplace, business operations, and civil rights, the champions of Progressivism argued that only the government had the power to curb the abuse and exploitative tactics of big business and fix the social problems that threatened American communities. The Progressive movement declared that if the government did not step in, America itself was in danger of crashing down in a storm of violence and chaos.

Though it took a number of years for the movement to gain a large amount of influence, Progressivism rose to prominence in the early 1900s. During the first two decades of the new century, municipal, state, and federal governments became much more involved in

movement was wide and varied. It included individuals such as President Theodore Roosevelt, woman suffrage advocate Alice Paul, journalist Upton Sinclair, social reformer Jane Addams, antialcohol evangelist Billy Sunday, Socialist Eugene V. Debs, and labor leader Mary Harris "Mother" Jones. Even though the causes and methods of these leaders and their organizations were unique and rarely aligned perfectly with each other, they shared a basic

addressing the nation's pressing economic and social problems. Numerous agencies and laws were created to fight poverty, pollution, exploitation of workers and immigrants, and political corruption. Lawmakers also passed far-reaching laws designed to address perceived social problems (such as the 18th Amendment, which ushered in the age of Prohibition) and areas of social injustice (such as the 19th Amendment, which gave women the right to vote).

Many of the laws and regulatory powers that the federal and state governments of America enacted during this era remain in force today, nearly a century after the Progressive Era came to an end. They govern the ways that Americans live, work, and conduct business. The continued importance of these laws and agencies to the fabric of American life provides compelling proof that the voices of the Progressive movement still echo in modern American society.

Chapter One

INCREASING INDUSTRIALISM

Though the Industrial Revolution was responsible for introducing a number of social issues into American life, it also marked a time of substantial development. A number of groundbreaking inventions, from automated weaving looms to the rise of steam engine travel, drastically improved the industry and infrastructure of the United States. The steam engine connected rural and urban Americans like never before. People of all social classes were able to travel quicker and more efficiently than anyone thought possible. As the business of manufacturing expanded and city populations grew, the United States stepped forward as one of the most industrialized countries in the world—following in England's footsteps after it experienced its own Industrial Revolution during the 1700s.

In England, many people were suspicious of the rapidly changing economy and way of life. They had been set in their ways for nearly 1,000 years; the United States, on the other hand, was a young country that had been separated from England for less than 100 years. Americans showed "widespread interest and approval … for any device that could augment [improve] labor and diminish the human work requirement," explained one historian,

[And] Americans were used to having change bring betterment, and they reached for [steam power and industrialization] with curiosity and eagerness. For the workers, machines could lighten the drudgery of a great many tasks that had formerly called for muscle power. For consumers, machines brought more goods, usually at lower prices. And for employers, they meant lower … labor costs.[2]

Though Americans were willing to change their lives dramatically—and quickly—industrialization took a while to really grow. The United States had historically been an agricultural country; there were few cities, and most people made a living from the land. Nonetheless, a few decades into the 1800s, there were massive and substantial changes across nearly all levels of American life. Steam travel, whether by train or boat, was opening the country, the growth of industry was contributing to the growth of cities, and the economy was flourishing with internal and international trade. These trends were magnified when the mid-19th century saw both a significant westward expansion and a huge increase in European immigration. This signaled that even greater changes were on the horizon.

Industry and Immigration

Railroads, the telegraph, and other creations of the industrial age greatly eased the opening and settlement of the American West. This, in turn, encouraged further investment in factories, railroads, telegraph systems, logging, mining, ranching, and farming. However, none of these developments could have taken place with such immediate success if it had not been for the tremendous influx of immigrants into America during the 19th century. These farmers, laborers, and merchants arrived by the millions, with numbers increasing with

each passing decade. They provided the nation's factories, coal mines, stockyards, and steel foundries with the workers they needed to match the thriving needs of an expanding national economy. Immigrants were also a major force in the settlement of the western wilderness. In short, they provided the young American nation with a massive infusion of hard work, ambition, and determination at a time when such assets were badly needed. Without their contributions, the industrialization and economic growth of America would have unfolded at a much slower pace.

The first large surge of immigrants who came to America in the 19th century fled poverty, starvation, and political oppression in northern and western Europe. From 1815 to 1860, more than 5 million immigrants, mainly coming from England, Ireland, Germany, and Scandinavia, made the difficult journey across the Atlantic Ocean to the United States. These new arrivals—along with immigrants from China and Mexico—were instrumental in the settlement of the West. Irish coal miners, Swedish farmers, Chinese railroad workers, Norwegian loggers, and German meatpackers all played an important role in converting the natural resources of the vast American West into fuel for the country's fast-growing economic engine. Immigrants worked alongside American-born citizens toward a shared goal: making America even

During the 1800s, America's railroads were one of its greatest national assets. They were constructed with help from workers of all races, including many immigrants.

better for their children.

After 1880, the ethnic makeup of new arrivals to America underwent a dramatic shift. The tide of immigration shifted to eastern and southern Europe, and by the close of the 19th century, immigrants from these regions accounted for nearly half of all immigrants to America. Immigrants from Italy, Poland, Hungary, Russia, and other eastern and southern European countries accounted for an even greater percentage of new arrivals in the first years of the 20th century. By 1900, roughly 26 million people in America—more than one-third of the country's entire population—were either immigrants or native-born Americans with at least one foreign-born parent. Many of them were employed as unskilled laborers. This means they were untrained in trades or arts that required specialized skills or knowledge, such as law, engineering, or science. As a result, they had little choice but to apply their sweat, hard work, and ambition in the factories of the nation's large cities, the farmlands of the Midwest and Great Plains, or the wild frontier in the West.

Money and Fitness

Around this same time, an influential idea called social Darwinism took root in the nation's boardrooms, newspaper offices, and statehouses. This idea was encouraged and spread by influential thinkers, such as American sociologist William Graham Sumner and British philosopher Herbert Spencer.

It was based on the research of scientist Charles Darwin, who developed a theory of natural evolution in the mid-19th century. His groundbreaking work is the foundation of all modern evolutionary study. Darwin's research proved that animals evolved over time and that creatures that were best adapted to survive (because of greater strength, speed, intelligence, or other adaptations) passed their genetic traits on to future generations. This concept is called survival of the fittest. Over time, Darwin argued, the fittest animals survived and passed these superior characteristics from generation to generation, which created a stronger, better-adapted species.

Spencer, Sumner, and other advocates of social Darwinism applied the concept of survival of the fittest to explain the dramatic differences in economic class that were emerging in America and other industrialized nations. They asserted that the fittest members of society were the ones who attained the greatest wealth or economic status. According to this argument, poor people

Influential British philosopher Herbert Spencer was one of the first people to describe social Darwinism. This idea spread across America during the late 1800s.

simply did not have the intelligence, ambition, or willpower to succeed in the new world of industrial commerce. This is a controversial idea, and it does not take into account other factors aside from wealth and economic prosperity.

The wealthy men who controlled America's railroads, factories, banks, and mills approved of and welcomed this theory, as did many middle-class Americans who had worked hard to carve out comfortable lives for themselves and their families. Social Darwinism not only allowed the wealthy to view themselves as the "best" citizens of the nation, it also gave them an excuse to ignore the terrible poverty afflicting millions of Americans. Social Darwinism also conformed to America's historical enthusiasm for individualism and self-improvement. All the country's most important founding documents, from the Declaration of Independence to the Constitution, "proclaimed the dignity and worth of the individual," wrote one historian. "The relentless spread of capitalism reaffirmed the individualist [idea], but with a new emphasis on each person's ownership of his or her labor."[3]

In modern times, the idea of social Darwinism is outdated and widely regarded as inappropriate. Economic success is not an evolutionary adaptation, and there are more aspects to human life than the amount of money in a bank account. Historians have frequently argued that the widespread belief in social Darwinism was simply a way for the wealthy and powerful to keep the lower classes down and increase their own profit margins.

Industrial Leaders

Some of America's most powerful men were not shy about expressing their belief in the importance of individuality in American capitalism. Not surprisingly, they also embraced the concept of social Darwinism. The famous industrialist Andrew Carnegie, one of the richest Americans in history, declared that humanity was able to advance "only through exceptional individuals … [It] is the leaders who do the new things that count, all these have been Individualistic to a degree beyond ordinary men and worked in perfect freedom; each and every one a character unlike anybody else; an original; gifted beyond most others of his kind, hence his leadership."[4]

Many of the country's political leaders shared Carnegie's beliefs. They condemned critics—especially poor ones—who dared to suggest that the huge contrast between the lives of America's wealthy industrialists and those of its poverty-stricken working class might actually be caused by greed and social injustice. In his 1901 memoir, for example, President Benjamin Harrison declared, "the [hatred] of the rich is mischievous. It [corrupts] the mind, poisons the heart and furnishes an excuse to crime. No poor man was

A Man of Steel

Andrew Carnegie was one of the most wealthy and influential businessmen in U.S. history. Born in Scotland in November 1835, he immigrated with his family to America in 1848. Carnegie first made his mark as a railroad supervisor and an intelligent investor. In 1872, he started investing and running companies in the steel business. Steel was the metal of the future: It was stronger, longer lasting, and more useful than iron. As Carnegie invested heavily in some of the nation's first steel foundries, his fortune grew exponentially.

Over the last two decades of the 19th century, Carnegie also diversified into many other industries, including coal, iron mining, and railroads. Carnegie used these properties to make his steel business even more profitable. In 1901, Carnegie sold the Carnegie Steel Company to another giant in American industry, J.P. Morgan, for $250 million. This is the equivalent of nearly $7 billion in the 21st century, which made this transaction one of the biggest business deals in U.S. history at the time.

After making this massive sale, Carnegie spent the rest of his life contributing to charitable causes and humanitarian work. Some of his biggest philanthropic contributions were to universities in his home country of Scotland and the city of Pittsburgh, Pennsylvania, American scientific research, and numerous other fields. By the time of Carnegie's death in 1919, he had changed his reputation. He transformed from a ruthless businessman and exploiter of workers to a charitable humanitarian.

Credited with the rapid expansion of the steel industry in America, Andrew Carnegie was one of the wealthiest men of the 19th century. His Scottish birth also means that he is one of the most successful immigrants of all time.

ever made richer or happier by it."[5]

These controversial beliefs contributed to the increasingly ruthless nature of American business in the 19th century. Many of the railroad tycoons, land developers, and factory owners who built their fortunes during this era did so by double-crossing business associates, bribing officials, and exploiting every last one of their underpaid and exhausted workers. Their behavior led ordinary Americans to refer to these powerful men as robber barons. Some historians have condemned the robber barons as cold-hearted monsters who made their riches by abusing the poor and vulnerable. Although they unquestionably engaged in inhumane practices, they also played an important role in building America into an economic superpower.

An Age of Prosperity

The themes of greed and selfishness became even more widespread during America's so-called Gilded Age, which unfolded during the last several decades of the 19th century. During these years, the nation's wealthiest men and women showed off their fortunes in ways that the country had never

seen before. Millions of Americans were struggling to support their families, but the rich were able to live in extreme comfort and luxury. One historian described the Gilded Age: "[W]hile children went unfed, the rich would spend tens of thousands of dollars on dinner parties where

A pioneer in the banking and finance industry, J.P. Morgan (left) was involved in hundreds of business deals, many of which were among the largest and most expensive of all time.

guests dined off solid-gold plates or, as at one given by Caroline Astor, would use sterling-silver [shovels] to dig through heaps of sand arranged on the table to find buried treasure troves of diamonds and rubies."[6]

The most notorious symbols of America's Gilded Age were the few dozen families that were able to take advantage of the rapid industrialization to achieve truly stunning levels of wealth and luxury. These fortunes were built by some of the most famous businessmen in U.S. history: steel pioneer Andrew Carnegie; financier J.P. Morgan; oil tycoon John D. Rockefeller; and railroad magnates Cornelius Vanderbilt, Jay Gould, and Edward H.

Harriman. These men and their families, icons of the Gilded Age, used their incredible riches to acquire huge mansions in the United States, sprawling estates in other countries, top-of-the-line yachts, private railway cars, and other highly visible signs of wealth.

Their fortunes were passed on to sons and daughters, who continued to surround themselves with extravagant luxury. All four of Vanderbilt's grandsons, for example, inherited millions of dollars, which they quickly used to acquire more mansions and land. All these homes were essentially palaces, but the one built by the youngest grandson, George, rivaled the greatest castles of Europe. His Biltmore

Seen by many historians as a symbol of excessive greed and extreme spending, the Biltmore Estate is considered today to be a cultural and historical landmark.

Estate, as it was known, was completed in 1895 in the heart of North Carolina's Blue Ridge Mountains. The 250-room mansion was the centerpiece of a 125,000-acre (50,585 ha) estate that included its own reservoirs, schools, dairy farms, and a hospital. After George Vanderbilt took up residence there, the Biltmore reportedly employed more workers than the entire U.S. Department of Agriculture.

Years of Discontent

In a time before radio, television, and the Internet, American newspapers and magazines provided extensive coverage of the lifestyles of America's rich, famous, and powerful. These periodicals were the primary sources of news and information for Americans in this era. They published accounts of fancy costume balls, expensive, wasteful dinner parties, and casual shopping sprees for expensive jewelry, clothes, and art. These reports were received with increasing anger and disapproval by a majority of the rest of the country.

Some of this anger came from feelings of jealousy, but many Americans were simply disgusted by such displays of wealth at a time when poverty and hopelessness dominated so many tenement slums and factory floors. Most working-class men and women at the turn of the century believed that the nation's wealthy elite were using their economic and political power to deliberately keep their fellow citizens in weaker and more desperate economic positions. They felt that the rules handed down by corporate bosses and their corrupt political allies were specifically constructed to give the lower classes little opportunity to improve their place in American society. John Mitchell, a union leader, described this feeling of hopelessness: "[The American laborer] understands that working men do not evolve into [wealthy] capitalists as boys evolve into men or as caterpillars evolve into butterflies."[7]

Progressive Origins

Near the beginning of the American Industrial Revolution, the first significant series of reforms of the post–Civil War era was the Granger movement. The movement began in 1867 when Oliver Hudson Kelley, a member of the federal Department of Agriculture, wanted to start an organization for rural farmers. These farmer groups were divided into sections called Granges, and the members were called Grangers. In the late 1860s, the Granges were primarily set up to educate and help the isolated members of the agricultural class. In the 1870s, though, local Grange organizations, concentrated in the upper Midwest and the South, became politically energized by the ruthless business practices of American railroads, banks, and grain elevator companies. They complained that high rail freight rates, high interest rates on bank loans, and high storage fees from grain elevators were likely to drive hardworking farmers out of business.

Frustrated and angry, the Grangers put political pressure on state legislatures to address these problems. As a result, a number of "Granger laws" were passed. These laws created a price ceiling on the rates that railroads and grain elevators could charge their customers. In response, railroads and other corporate interests challenged the Granger laws in court. Rural farmers won a decisive victory when the Supreme Court ruled in 1877 that states were allowed to regulate private industry when the public good was at risk. By the mid-1870s, the national Grange membership had reached upward of 800,000 members.

Though the influence of the Granger movement declined near the end of the century, many of the problems that had sparked the birth of the Granger movement still remained. In the early 1890s, a new movement to fight back against big business and political corruption arose out of America's heartland. The Populist movement developed in the agricultural communities of the South, Great Plains, and Midwest.

A People's Party

Formed after groups of rural farmers, similar to the Grangers, dissolved and lost power, many of these members reorganized into a political party called the Populist or People's Party. This was supposed to be an alternative option for people who were dissatisfied with both Republicans and Democrats. They believed that the federal government had a moral and legal duty to limit corporate power and address other problems of the industrial age. To create new laws, the Populists tried to get members of their party elected to local, state, and federal government positions. They ran on the Omaha Platform, which called for federal ownership of the nation's railroad, telegraph, and telephone industries to ensure fair prices for all citizens. They also lobbied for changes to the American monetary system that would benefit farmers and working-class people.

Another Populist priority was the establishment of a new income tax system, in which poor Americans would pay a lower percentage of their income in taxes than rich Americans. In addition, the People's Party wanted to create a series of new restrictions on foreign immigration into the United States because they viewed immigrants as a threat to the jobs and wages of native-born Americans. Political corruption was another major target of the Populists. Leaders of the movement fought, for example, to reform the civil service system so that qualified workers, rather than people with political connections, would fill government jobs. Populists were also some of the first major voices to call for direct election of representatives to the U.S. Senate.

In 1892, the People's Party made a huge push for political power: A Populist candidate was on the ballot for the presidency. Though their choice, James B. Weaver, got just 22 electoral votes, he won more than 1 million popular votes and managed to get the Populist name widespread. Over the next several years, the party had candidates successfully run for seats in state government and the House of Representatives, and in 1894, it even managed to claim some offices in the Senate. In the 1896 presidential election, the People's Party endorsed Democratic presidential candidate William Jennings Bryan, who shared many of their political beliefs. Bryan lost to Republican William McKinley, however, and the Populist Party faded away over the next few years due to its failure to expand beyond its largely rural base.

Despite its short life span, many historians believe that the Populist movement helped shape the Progressive movement, which rose out of the Populist Party in the early 20th century. Progressivism in the South and Great

Though James B. Weaver was never a serious candidate for the presidency, he did win over the support of more than 1 million Americans. His Populist Party influenced the later Progressive movement.

Plains states, where Populism had been strongest, focused most heavily on economic issues that affected farmers and rural communities. Northern Progressives concentrated on urban poverty, child labor, and other "city" problems, while agrarian Progressives aimed their fire at the exploitative business practices of railroads, meat packers, and other industrial giants upon which farmers and ranchers relied for their livelihoods.

Labor activists and Populists were among the most vocal critics of American industrialization, but they did not stand alone. Many educated, middle-class Americans also felt outraged over the huge divide between the nation's wealthy elite and the rest of its citizens. They felt that this income gap completely disregarded both American and Christian ideals of equality and compassion.

"Deeply Stirred"

During the age of industrialization, the anger, frustration, and hopelessness that America's poor and working class experienced were creating political ripples. The efforts of the Grangers and the Populist Movement had created a few waves, but they did not achieve any significant reforms. Once America's middle class became engaged in the issues of poverty, corruption, and social justice, however, the movement toward Progressivism became a raging storm on the political ocean.

Some middle-class Americans joined the Progressive movement out of a desire to preserve their comfortable, privileged lifestyle. They believed their peaceful middle-class existence would be threatened if America did not implement reforms to address its festering problems of poverty, corruption, and class division. They reasoned that if moderate reforms to address the worst corporate abuses and slum conditions were passed, the radical voices calling for revolution would simply fade away. They would be able to sleep soundly, secure in the knowledge that their stable daily lives would be there for them when they woke up.

Many other middle-class Americans, however, joined the Progressive movement out of a genuine sense of moral obligation to the poor. American-born white families made up a huge portion of the middle class at the beginning of the 20th century. Few immigrants, African Americans, or other minorities of this era possessed the financial and educational resources or social freedom to achieve a middle-class level of security and comfort. Many white members of the middle class saw this state of affairs as acceptable—and even desirable. However, the belief that one had a moral duty to aid the less fortunate had been a founding principle of American society since colonial times, and it remained an important part of American self-identity.

This sense of moral responsibility

was supported in large part by the powerful religious beliefs of most middle-class families in America. The greed and waste of the Gilded Age deeply offended these men and women, who had been raised on biblical themes that emphasized fellowship, community, and good works for the benefit of all God's children. By the start of the 20th century, large segments of the nation's middle class were part of a so-called Social Gospel movement. This movement was based on the belief that it was time "to return to American life an emphasis on Protestant morals that had been lost in an economic system that worshipped [money] more than Christ ... Progressivism for such people became a mission, a holy war, a crusade for virtue and the betterment of mankind."[8]

As the 20th century began, middle-class Americans were getting more involved with the problems confronting the nation, especially the problems facing the poorest Americans. According to Kansas newspaper editor William Allen White,

> We ... were deeply stirred. Our sympathies were responding excitedly to a sense of injustice that had become a part of the new glittering, gaudy machine age. Machines of steel and copper and wood and stone, and bookkeeping and managerial talent, were creating a new order. It looked glamorous. It seemed permanent; yet, because

> someway the masses of the world, not the proletariat but the middle class, had qualms and squeamish doubts about the way things were going, discontent rose in the hearts of the people and appeared in world politics.[9]

Early Reformation

This widespread unhappiness with the state of American society forced lawmakers to pass several reformative laws in the 1880s and 1890s. The first major reform was the 1883 Pendleton Civil Service Act, which was named after and supported by Ohio senator George H. Pendleton. This law created the foundation for the modern civil service system by tearing down the "spoils system" that had been the norm in American politics for more than half a century.

Under the spoils system, many government jobs were filled by friends and supporters of politicians rather than by qualified applicants. The Pendleton Act did not completely outlaw this practice, but it did eliminate some of the most corrupt elements of the spoils system. For example, the act provided for open exams for applicants for government jobs and made it illegal for lawmakers to force civil servants to help their political campaigns. Though it originally covered just 10 percent of all federal jobs, it has been expanded repeatedly over the years to cover more.

Other efforts at reform were not so

successful, however. In 1887, for example, Congress created the Interstate Commerce Commission (ICC) to regulate the railroad industry. The arrival of the ICC was an important milestone, because it was the nation's first federal regulatory agency, but it was given only limited power to enforce its rules. Because of this, many railroads continued to charge inflated freight rates and engage in other ruthless business practices.

Other laws meant to put controls on the power of America's corporate giants also proved ineffective. One prominent example of this was the 1890 Sherman Antitrust Act, which was named for its chief sponsor, Senator John Sherman of Ohio. The law was meant to prevent a single trust, or related group of companies, from dominating a given industry. It failed miserably. In 1895, for instance, federal authorities charged the American Sugar Refining Company with violating the act. Even though the company controlled 98 percent of the nation's sugar production at that time, the pro-business U.S. Supreme Court ruled in *United States v. E.C. Knight Company* that the act applied strictly to the sale of goods, not to the manufacturing or production of goods. After this ruling, neither government regulators nor corporations paid much attention to the act, and it was largely ineffective for decades.

Despite these disappointments, the thirst for genuine reform of American politics and business did not subside. Instead, the calls for reform became even greater as the 19th century came to a close. During the last two decades, Americans were rocked by bitter, and sometimes violent, labor disputes in numerous industries and a four-year economic depression that began in 1893.

A Riot

One violent confrontation between workers and management during America's age of industrialization took place in Chicago, Illinois: the Haymarket Riot of 1886. The unease began on May 3, when owners of the McCormick Harvesting Machine Company convinced police to break up local support of a nationwide strike that had been called by union leaders seeking better wages and shorter workweeks. When the police arrived, they immediately clashed with striking workers and their supporters. Violence broke out, one striker was killed, and several strikers were injured.

One day later, a group of organized labor leaders took advantage of public outrage about the police interference and organized another protest meeting, this time at Haymarket Square. Though Chicago's mayor issued a statement proclaiming that it was a peaceful meeting, the police arrived in force near the end of the demonstration. After they tried to disperse the protestors, one unidentified protestor threw a homemade bomb into their

In the early years of the Progressive movement, strikers were sometimes subjected to violent suppression by governmental forces. The Haymarket Riot, depicted here, was deadly for both police and workers.

ranks. The explosion and the resulting violence caused the deaths of 7 police officers and between 4 and 8 civilians, and nearly 100 people were wounded between both sides.

Eight men, who were known to be leaders of extreme labor groups, were arrested, tried, and convicted of murder in the aftermath of the tragedy. Four of them were executed, and another committed suicide in prison. Meanwhile, other labor leaders tried to distance themselves from the violence, which terrified many Americans. Still, many workers, union activists, left-wing political radicals, and opponents of the death penalty asserted that the alleged murderers had been convicted on flimsy evidence, and in 1893, Illinois governor John Peter Altgeld declared that the judge had not given them a fair trial. The three living men were then pardoned.

Striking Backward and Forward

The most notorious clash between labor and management was the 1894 Pullman Strike in Chicago. This dispute started when the owners of the Pullman Palace Car Company sharply reduced employee wages—but made no changes to the rent costs of the company-owned homes in which the workers lived. The company also refused to drop the prices of goods at their company stores. Pullman workers were outraged. Labor organizer Eugene V. Debs, president of the American Railway Union (ARU), quickly organized more than 100,000 workers in a strike that spread to other railroads in the western half of the country. As railroad operations ground to a halt, railroad owners and businesses dependent on rail service begged the federal government to intervene. President Grover Cleveland ordered federal troops into Illinois.

After several weeks of violent clashes between law enforcement and the strikers, the strike was broken by the beginning of August. Moreover, Eugene V. Debs and other leading figures of the ARU were arrested and charged. Many Americans approved of President Cleveland's intervention and sided with management in the Pullman dispute. Others, however, were outraged by the events in Chicago. They interpreted the outcome of the Pullman Strike as clear evidence that hardworking but poor Americans remained no match for the powerful corporate giants that were in control of the nation's politics and economy.

As the final years of the 19th century ticked away, the calls for reform of America's economic, political, and social fabric became steadily louder. Even the rich and powerful industrialists who controlled the country's factories, shipyards, and railroads began to take notice of the rising protests. They were troubled by a steady escalation in labor disputes across the country, as well as growing public anxiety about poverty, urban quality of life, and political corruption. Some men, such as famed attorney Clarence Darrow, warned that ugly class divisions in America threatened the very existence of the country: "If [the country's collapse] shall come in the lightning and tornado of civil war, the same as forty years ago," Darrow said in 1895, "when you then look ... over the ruin and desolation, remember the long years in which the storm was rising, and do not blame the thunderbolt."[10]

As America's industrialists and politicians assessed the severity of the gathering threat, the most sensible of them followed Darrow's words. They remembered the earlier decades of the 19th century, when a wide range of political reformers and radicals had protested against the abuses of industrial America. Back then, the corporations had ruthlessly used their political connections and economic strength to neutralize the early reformers—such as the Grangers, Populists, and unionists—who tried to bring about major changes to American laws and society. As the 19th century drew to a close,

America's Businessman

The richest man in America during the Progressive Era was industrialist John D. Rockefeller. Born in upstate New York in July 1839, Rockefeller became an investor and

Building his fortune in oil, John D. Rockefeller is a symbol of many things to modern Americans. He was simultaneously ruthless, charitable, disliked, and respected. Above all, he was wealthy; modern experts estimate that he is one of the richest men who ever lived.

a new generation of reformers rose to carry on their campaigns of social and economic justice. These activists were far more influential than the Grangers, Populists, and early unionists had ever been. Shaken by this

speculator in the oil industry in the 1860s, and in 1870, he established the Standard Oil Company. Over the next several years, Rockefeller used alliances with other powerful businessmen in the railroad and oil industries to force dozens of other refiners to sell their operations to him or go out of business.

In 1881, Standard Oil was turned into the first major American trust company, and it accounted for more than 90 percent of the oil refined in the United States. By the end of the 1890s, Standard Oil dominated all phases of the oil industry—exploration, refining, and marketing—and Rockefeller's Standard Oil Trust was the richest and most feared company in America.

In 1906, President Theodore Roosevelt aggressively campaigned to dissolve the Standard Oil Trust and weaken its stranglehold over the oil industry. Charging Rockefeller and Standard with a wide range of unfair and illegal business practices, Roosevelt moved to break the trust into smaller independent companies. Rockefeller fought back in the courts, but in May 1911, the U.S. Supreme Court ruled against him. By the end of the year, Standard Oil had been dismantled into a number of smaller—and less powerful—companies.

For much of his business career, the American public hated Rockefeller because of his ruthless practices. In the 1910s and 1920s, though, his generous philanthropic gifts in the areas of education, art, and scientific research made him more popular. It has been estimated that throughout his lifetime, John D. Rockefeller donated more than $530 million to various charitable causes.

knowledge, some industrialists and lawmakers decided that they needed to make some changes if they hoped to keep Darrow's grim warning from coming true.

Chapter Two

SOCIETY AND POLITICS

As the 20th century approached, the United States was at a crossroads. Two sides—the Progressives and the industrialists—were set up to furiously fight each other over America's future. During the earliest years of the 1900s, the reformers won many political and social battles. The issues of poverty, political corruption, unequal rights for women, and the exploitation of immigrant workers were some of the chief targets for the Progressive movement in the new century. To attack these issues, Progressive leaders went back to some of the root causes, such as overcrowded cities, unregulated industry, and a lack of political oversight. In the early 20th century, the movement was widely successful in addressing a number of these concerns.

One area where the Progressives made little impact was another longstanding issue in the United States: race relations. Despite the conclusion of the American Civil War and the end of slavery, African Americans were still considered second-class citizens. They were frequently subjected to discrimination, violence, and exploitative practices. The Progressive movement, however, left these issues mostly unattended. Many leaders even considered continued segregation to be the best option for the nation. The decision by most Progressives to leave African Americans by the wayside is one of the movement's most shameful aspects.

Urban Expansion

The Industrial Revolution began changing the United States from a society of farmers and rural towns to one of factory workers and sprawling cities. However, agriculture was still an important part of the economy, and millions of families continued to support themselves by raising crops or livestock even after the emergence of railroads, telegraphs, factories, and steel foundries in the 19th century. With each passing decade, though, the percentage of Americans who lived in cities—where the industrial jobs were located— grew larger.

At the beginning of the 20th century, the nation's largest cities housed about 21 million Americans, roughly 28 percent of the total population. By the 1930s, more than 59 million people, nearly half of the total U.S. population, lived in large metropolitan areas. The dramatic growth of America's cities came from two places: the migration of citizens from rural to urban areas, and the arrival of immigrants from overseas.

In terms of migration within the United States, native-born people of all races were attracted to the industrial jobs that the cities offered. Northern industrialized cities, such as New York; Chicago; Cleveland, Ohio; Detroit, Michigan; and Philadelphia, Pennsylvania, were particularly popular destinations. The cities of the North held the possibility of a better life for poor, rural whites, and

Despite the abolition of slavery, racism was still prevalent across America during the late 19th century. Jim Crow laws were used to keep African Americans below whites.

they offered even more improvement for African Americans living in the South. Black southerners had endured decades of poverty and humiliation as a result of discriminatory Jim Crow laws in the South, and they were anxious to escape. "As long as Jim Crow ruled the South," one historian wrote, "that system of segregation, subordination, and terror created powerful incentives for leaving and staying away."[11] The first great wave of migratory, rural, southern African Americans came to the industrial cities of the North beginning in the 1890s, and these waves became more powerful in each of the next three decades.

The movement from rural America to the great industrial cities occurred at the same time that foreign immigrants were entering the United States in greater numbers than ever before. Many of these immigrants settled close to each other in cities. Surrounded by neighbors with the same cultural backgrounds as themselves, they could practice their religions, speak their native languages, and engage in other ethnic traditions in peace. Across the country, city populations swelled higher.

A Desperate Life

The new arrivals to the industrial cities provided essential labor for factories, stockyards, construction companies, and other industries. Despite this, the urban conditions in which most of these workers lived and toiled were terrible. American cities simply did not have the capacity to keep up with the population explosions they were experiencing. One historian pointed out that in 1840, Chicago "had been a village of log huts around Fort Dearborn holding scarcely five thousand residents; by 1890, it was a city of 165 square miles with one million residents, increasing by some fifty thousand each year, transforming pastures seemingly overnight into swarming tenements."[12]

Overcrowding reached epidemic proportions in every large city. Families crammed together in tenement slums that became breeding grounds for disease and crime. Factories and sewage systems, meanwhile, dumped alarming amounts of pollution into the air and water because there were no laws against such practices at the time. Residents became accustomed to these terrible living conditions, but visitors were shocked and disgusted. Author Hamlin Garland wrote that the memory of his first glimpse of late–19th century Chicago would always haunt him: "[I shall] never forget the feeling of dismay with which … I perceived from the [rail] car window a huge smoke-cloud which embraced the whole eastern horizon, for this, I was told, was the soaring banner of the great and gloomy inland metropolis."[13]

The poor living conditions in working-class neighborhoods were torture for fathers and mothers who had hoped to provide better lives for their families. Unskilled and semiskilled industrial workers were paid such small wages that they had little hope of securing

Because of the rapid expansion of industry, city populations began to grow faster than the cities themselves. This resulted in overcrowded tenements and homelessness.

better accommodations elsewhere in the city, let alone out in the comparatively safe, spacious, and comfortable lands outside the city. In fact, the challenge of economic survival was so great that many families had to rely on a household economy in which all family members worked—including children. Millions of families were forced to send their children to work in factories at inappropriately young ages. By the close of the 19th century, exploitation of children for labor was a widespread feature of America's industrial cities.

Reforming the Machine

All these problems were made worse by the widespread political corruption that infected nearly every large municipal government. Fraud, bribery, and other profit-making activities were so commonplace in city governments that officials and residents alike came to see corruption as the usual state of affairs. Lawmakers and officials claimed that accepting bribes and handing out

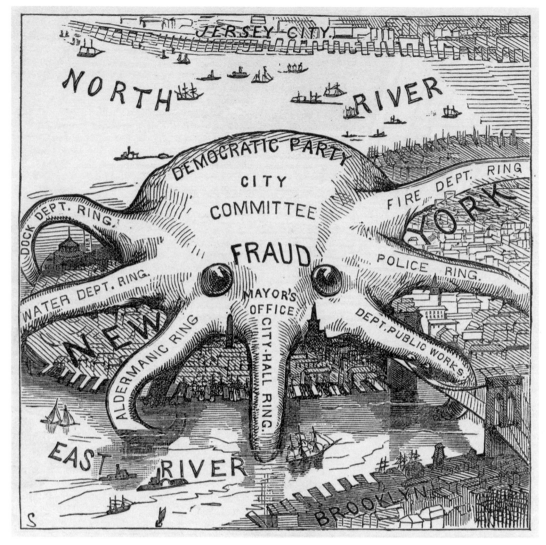

This 19th-century illustration is symbolic of the corrupt political operations that infested most large American cities.

political favors was nothing more than taking advantage of their opportunities. For years, many residents had to accept the existence of corrupt political parties and government agencies simply because their influence seemed too powerful to resist. Political allianc-

es with business interests were soon named the political machine, and thousands of corrupt officials benefited at the expense of the taxpayers.

In the Progressive Era, however, these political machines came under a sustained attack by various reform leaders. Investigations of fraud and bribery increased, and some cities passed important reformative legislation to improve the performance and responsiveness of municipal agencies. Progressives demanded that municipal governments separate themselves from businesses.

City governments were by no means the only focus of political reform. Corruption at the state and federal level was also a widespread problem, and Progressives acted decisively in this area as well. Reform-minded governors, such as Hiram Johnson of California and Robert M. La Follette of Wisconsin, promoted wider citizen participation in the electoral process. They knew that if ordinary citizens received a greater voice in selecting their representatives and making laws, the influence of powerful corporate interests and corrupt lawmakers would be reduced.

Efforts to usher in a new era of direct democracy included the introduction of new political tools. The initiative, the recall, the referendum, and the primary came into American politics early in the 20th century, and they have persisted ever since. Many of these measures were first approved in western states and gradually moved eastward. The initiative gave voters the power to pass legislation on their own by putting legal propositions on voting ballots, rather than depending on corrupt, incompetent, or hostile lawmakers in the state legislatures. This became an important tool of the Prohibition and suffrage movements in the 1900s and 1910s. The recall allowed voters to remove elected officials from office in special elections. The referendum gave voters the power to either approve or disapprove their state legislature's actions. The primary neutralized the power of political machines by taking the selection of political candidates out of the hands of party

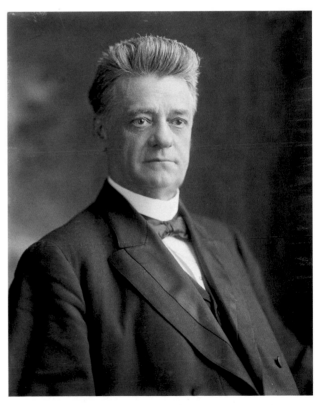

One of the most influential Progressives, Robert M. La Follette passed new laws in Wisconsin and fought for reformative legislation on the federal level for many years.

leaders and placing it into the hands of voting citizens.

The Progressive campaign to reduce corruption and secret deals even extended to the way that U.S. senators were elected. For more than a century, U.S. senators had been elected or appointed by state legislatures rather than by popular vote. Progressives changed this by successfully campaigning for a constitutional amendment that would provide for the direct election of senators by the people. This amendment—the 17th Amendment to the Constitution—was ratified by the states in 1913 and was first put into effect in the 1914 elections.

Vocal Critics

Some of the early leaders in the crusades to address America's massive urban problems were Progressive reformers who were affiliated with churches and private charities. Their efforts to enlist the support of middle-class Americans in their cause were greatly aided by two factors. One factor was the growing belief, within middle-class homes and neighborhoods, that corporate exploitation of workers had to be reformed and poor Americans deserved a helping hand. The other factor—which played a major role in shaping middle-class opinion—was the work of journalists who were called muckrakers. This was an insulting term used by President Theodore Roosevelt to describe them as people who only looked at the bad parts—the "muck"—of American life.

Magazines and newspapers reached the historical height of their power during the Progressive Era. They were the primary source of news in the age before television and the Internet, and revolutionary innovations in transportation and communication during the second half of the 1800s gave them greater reach than they had ever experienced before. Progressives led many of these magazines and newspapers, and they supported journalists who relentlessly exposed the dark underside of America's industrial expansion. Crusading journalists such as Henry Demarest Lloyd, Ray Stannard Baker, Ida Tarbell, Charles Edward Russell, Frank Norris, David Graham Phillips, and Lincoln Steffens filled the pages of *Atlantic Monthly*, *McClure's*, *American Magazine*, *Cosmopolitan*, *Everybody's Magazine*, and other prominent publications with shocking accounts of corporate ruthlessness, urban hopelessness, and political corruption.

Book publishers added their voices as well. They printed important works such as *How the Other Half Lives: Studies among the Tenements of New York* (1890), a book by reformer Jacob Riis that forced Americans to confront the revolting conditions in the urban slums. Other influential books included Steffens's *The Shame of the Cities* (1904), which revealed the corruption of city governments in New York and Chicago; Norris's novel *The Octopus: A Story of California* (1901), which condemned greedy railroads; and Upton Sinclair's *The Jungle* (1906), which shocked Americans with its descriptions of the brutality and unhealthy conditions found in the nation's meatpacking industry.

These articles and books triggered numerous investigations of corrupt political and business interests. They also helped build public support for local, state, and federal laws designed to address the problems of child labor, hazardous working conditions, unsanitary and overcrowded slums, and exploited immigrants. Sinclair's *The Jungle* was directly responsible for the creation of two of the most important laws of the entire Progressive Era. The Pure Food and Drug Act and the Meat Inspection Act, both of which were signed into law by President Theodore Roosevelt in 1906, were created to address the outrage that Americans expressed after reading Sinclair's book.

Women at Work

The effort of America's muckraking journalists inspired the larger Progressive movement that swept across the country during the first two decades of the 20th century. Within this movement, educated, white, middle-class women were a particularly influential group. "They not only were strongly moved by the moral and ethical dilemmas of their time," explained one scholar, "but also found an outlet for their talents working among the poor that the broader society denied them."[14] Taking advantage of the widespread belief that women were America's moral guardians and homemakers, female reformers argued that they had an ethical duty to make their voices heard on public sanitation, education, poverty, and other issues that affected families. Their message was embraced by other women, who joined the Progressive cause in huge numbers during the 1890s and the 1900s.

These women activists were responsible for creating and nurturing some of the country's most prominent reform-oriented associations. Organizations such as the Women's Trade Union League, the Women's Christian Temperance Union, and the National Consumers' League joined other Progressive organizations in fighting against a wide assortment of social issues. These reform efforts targeted trends such as alcohol abuse and the exploitation of women and children in the garment industry. Protestant ministers were a particularly important ally in these efforts. Troubled by the corruption and poverty of industrial America, they preached a Social Gospel message that called on church members to find salvation by reaching out to the less fortunate.

Women also were essential in the development and maintenance of settlement houses, which were designed to help struggling native-born families and immigrant families adjust to the challenging life in industrialized America. The first of these facilities sprouted in American cities in the late 1880s and early 1890s. By 1910, more than 400 settlement houses had been established in cities across the country. The settlement houses helped the poor learn how they could potentially improve their lives. Settlement house leaders also lobbied city and state officials to improve workplace

More Than a Homemaker

Jane Addams, founder of the revolutionary Hull House, was born in Cedarville, Illinois, on September 6, 1860. Raised in comfortable surroundings by parents who taught tolerance and compassion for others, Addams decided to open a settlement house in Chicago after touring similar facilities in Europe. She and fellow Progressive activist Ellen Gates Starr opened Hull House in one of Chicago's poor neighborhoods in 1889, and over the next two decades, it became the nation's most famous private provider of social programs for poor and working-class families. It also served as the blueprint for hundreds of other settlement houses that appeared in dozens of American cities during the Progressive Era.

The success of Hull House vaulted Addams into a position of national prominence. Addams wrote numerous books explaining her Progressive ideals, and she went on lecture tours around the country to talk about the expanding establishment of settlement houses. She also served in leadership positions in important reform organizations, such as the National Conference of Social Work and the International Congress of Women. She spoke out on behalf of woman suffrage and assisted in the founding of the National Association for the Advancement of Colored People (NAACP) in 1909 and the American Civil Liberties Union (ACLU) in 1920.

A dedicated pacifist, Addams strongly opposed U.S. entry into World War I. In 1919, she was elected the first president of the Women's International League for Peace and Freedom, an organization dedicated to international peace efforts. Her work in this area led critics to accuse her of supporting disloyal and anti-American political beliefs. Not bothered by these allegations, Addams remained an energetic peace activist and social reformer. In 1931, she was awarded the Nobel Peace Prize for her many works. She died in Chicago on May 21, 1935.

safety; increase trash collection; expand sewage systems; eliminate child labor in urban factories; and increase welfare benefits for widows, the elderly, and impoverished citizens.

The most famous of the nation's settlement houses was Chicago's Hull House, which was founded by Jane Addams in 1889. The model for many later settlement houses, Hull House provided services to the immigrant and poor families that crowded the tenements of Chicago's West Side. As the Progressive movement gained strength,

Hull House, shown here, was the most successful American settlement house. Jane Addams became an influential Progressive leader because of her work there.

Addams and her mostly female associates at Hull House established an array of social programs for working-class families that were not yet available from state or federal governments. These included kindergarten and day care facilities for the children of working mothers; an employment bureau; libraries; an art gallery; meeting places for trade unions; recreational activities for young, single women; and classes in English, citizenship, music, art, and theater.

In many cases, the advocacy efforts of settlement house reformers made a real difference in people's lives. Settlement house activists were essential in convincing legislators to establish separate courts for juvenile offenders in 32 states and mothers' pension programs in 18 states by the end of 1913. Lillian Wald of New York's Henry Street Settlement House was instrumental in the 1912 creation of the Federal Children's Bureau, the first federal agency charged with monitoring and investigating child labor in American industries. Addams, Wald, and other settlement house reformers also generated vital public and legislative support for the 1916 passage of the Keating-Owen Child Labor Act, the first federal law restricting child labor. It limited the working hours of children and prohibited the interstate sale of goods that had been produced by child labor.

Working for Women

Women's rights were another major cause for the Progressive movement. Many women wanted to see changes such as increased social acceptance of divorce. These reformers were also at the forefront of the birth control movement. Advocates of birth control and legal, regulated abortion became a powerful political force in the 1910s under the leadership of Margaret Sanger, who founded the organization that eventually became the Planned Parenthood Federation of America in 1921. Sanger and other similar activists wanted the government to invest in educating the American public—specifically women—about birth control methods and how to avoid an unwanted pregnancy.

Birth control was a controversial issue in America, but it was overshadowed during the Progressive Era by the issue of woman suffrage. The struggle to give women the right to vote had been waged since 1848, when Lucretia Mott and Elizabeth Cady Stanton organized the first woman suffrage convention in New York. Though the Seneca Falls Convention made a few waves in 1848, the movement enjoyed little widespread success until the beginning of the 20th century, when woman suffrage received a huge boost from Progressives who believed that women could provide the necessary votes to pass Progressive legislation.

By 1910, four western states—Wyoming, Colorado, Utah, and Idaho—had given women the right to vote, in part because of the support of prominent men such as Democratic senator Robert Owen of Oklahoma and the Progressive Kansas newspaper editor William Allen White. Two years later, former president Theodore Roosevelt—a great political hero of the Progressive Era—abandoned his previous caution in supporting woman suffrage. As the presidential nominee of the Progressive—also called the Bull Moose—Party, he enthusiastically endorsed the idea. His 1912 campaign to reclaim the White House failed, but Roosevelt and the Progressive Party became the first major American political party to welcome women as equals. Women were placed in leadership positions in the party and played important roles in the campaign, and Jane Addams was even given the platform to vocally support Roosevelt's nomination at the party convention.

In the mid-1910s, divisions within the suffrage movement threatened to derail the efforts to secure voting rights for all adult women citizens across America. The protests of woman suffrage advocates, such as the political radical Alice Paul, kept the issue alive. "[T]o me it was shocking that a government of men could look with such extreme contempt on a movement that was asking nothing except such a simple little thing as the right to vote,"[15] Paul later recalled. She and other suffragettes, as they were named, waged a relentless campaign of demonstrations, hunger strikes, and picketing outside the White House in the hope of getting President Woodrow Wilson to drop his neutral stance on the issue. This continued pressure, combined with the steady efforts of more moderate groups, such as the National American Woman Suffrage Association (NAWSA), finally convinced the Wilson administration to endorse woman suffrage.

Wilson's support for suffrage had an immediate impact on Congress, which had previously done its best to ignore the issue. On May 21, 1919, the 19th Amendment to the U.S. Constitution (widely known

Elizabeth Cady Stanton was one of the most important early supporters of woman suffrage in America.

Speaking Out to Support Women

One of the leading supporters of woman suffrage in the U.S. Senate was Oklahoma's Robert Owen, a Progressive Democrat. In a 1910 speech, Owen highlighted the benefits of woman suffrage in the western states that had passed suffrage laws:

> The man is usually better informed with regard to state government, but women are better informed about house government, and she can learn state government with as much [ease] as he can learn how to instruct children, properly feed and clothe the household, care for the sick, play on the piano, or make a house beautiful ... Every evil prophecy against granting the suffrage has failed. The public men of Colorado, Wyoming, Utah, and Idaho give it a [warm] support.

> The testimony is universal:

> First ... [women] still love their homes and children just the same as ever, and are better able to protect themselves and their children because of the ballot ... It has made women broader and greatly increased the understanding of the community at large of the problems of good government; of proper sanitation, of pure food, [of] clean water, and all such matters in which intelligent women would naturally take an interest.[1]

1. Quoted in David M. Kennedy and Thomas Bailey, *The American Spirit: U.S. History as Seen by Contemporaries, vol. 2: Since 1865.* Boston, MA: Wadsworth, 2010, pp. 215–216.

as the Susan B. Anthony Amendment, named after the women's rights advocate) granting women the right to vote passed the U.S. House of Representatives. Two weeks later, the measure passed the U.S. Senate and went to the states for ratification. If approved by three-quarters of the states, the proposed amendment would become federal law. Legislatures in Michigan and Wisconsin were the first to ratify the amendment, and in the ensuing months, many other states followed suit. Finally, on August 18, 1920, Tennessee became the 36th state to ratify the amendment, which pushed the 19th Amendment above the three-quarters threshold. After years of struggle and disappointment, American women finally had the right to vote.

Against Alcohol

Some Progressives also joined the long and bitter war against alcohol consumption in American society. Not all Progressives supported campaigns for temperance (moderate use of alcohol) or outright bans, or prohibitions, on alcohol production and consumption. Those who did support these measures, though, believed that alcohol abuse made life worse for countless families, especially in the poor tenement neighborhoods of the big cities. Some Prohibition activists even saw alcohol as a moral threat to the future of the nation. As one minister stated, "[Liquor is] the open sore of this land … the most fiendish, corrupt … institution that ever crawled out of the slime."[16]

America's leading groups that campaigned to make alcohol consumption illegal, such as the Women's Christian Temperance Union and the Anti-Saloon League, had been founded in the late 19th century. Despite the efforts of early Prohibition leaders Frances Willard, Carry Nation, and Howard Hyde Russell, they made little progress until the late 1890s. As the 20th century approached, public anxiety about immigrants, chaotic cities, and a long economic depression brought a new wave of supporters for Prohibition. One scholar explained their reasoning:

If cities were choking in industrial smoke and shameful immorality, if strange, new peoples and alien languages and political philosophies cast an eerie cloud over traditional America, there had to be reasons. If economic misery strangled the nation, if families split apart, if crime increased and suicides were on the rise, there had to be answers. For many, the greatest of the reasons was liquor; the most urgent of the answers was to wipe it out.[17]

Popular Christian evangelist Billy Sunday, one of the most famous Prohibition champions of the Progressive Era, summed up this view in his famous "Booze Sermon": "The saloon is the sum of all villainies. It is worse than war or [disease]. It is the crime of crimes. It is parent of crimes and the mother of sins."[18]

Though only a few states had outright bans on the sale of alcohol at the outset of the 20th century, a number of southern states passed Prohibition laws in spite of opposition from liquor producers, liquor distributors, and working-class Americans who resented being lectured about how they spent their few leisure hours. Efforts to pass federal Prohibition laws also gained additional support due to the tireless efforts of Sunday and Anti-Saloon League leaders, such as Wayne Wheeler, Bishop James Cannon Jr., and Purley A. Baker. "The vices of the cities have been the undoing of past empires and civilizations," Baker declared in 1914. "Already some of our cities are … manipulated by the [destructive] unAmerican drink traffic

… If our Republic is to be saved the liquor traffic must be destroyed."[19]

Despite the rising call for decreased alcohol consumption, politicians remained wary of voicing support for Prohibition, even though it was popular with large numbers of both evangelicals and Progressives. The beer, wine, and liquor industries were major parts of the American economy, and they were also large contributors to many political campaigns. Politicians at every level recognized that Prohibition was deeply unpopular with significant numbers of American voters. All three presidents of the Progressive Era—Theodore Roosevelt, William Taft, and Woodrow Wilson—tried to avoid taking any stance at all on the issue. "My experience with prohibitionists," admitted Roosevelt, "is … that the best way to deal with them is to ignore them."[20]

Pro-Prohibition?

In the 1910s, the political power of the Prohibition movement became clear to all. Sweeping new laws were passed against alcohol in even more states, and many legislators who opposed Prohibition were voted out of office across the country. Lawmakers in Washington, D.C., quickly responded to the shift in momentum. In 1917, Congress passed a proposed constitutional amendment prohibiting the manufacture, distribution, or sale of alcoholic beverages. It then sent it to the individual states for ratification. Little more than one year later, Nebraska became the 36th state to ratify the amendment, which put it over the three-quarters requirement. In early 1919, the Prohibition amendment officially became the 18th Amendment to the U.S. Constitution. On January 16, 1920, Prohibition took effect across the land.

Advocates of Prohibition rejoiced at their victory, but enforcement of the new law was an utter failure from the beginning. An underground industry devoted to providing alcohol to Americans who opposed Prohibition sprang up virtually overnight. People who manufactured, smuggled, and sold alcohol were called bootleggers. By the mid-1920s, bootleggers were supporting huge numbers of illegal drinking establishments— known as speakeasies—that could be found in every American city. These establishments ranged from glamorous clubs with live entertainment to filthy barrooms with a few scattered tables. Some were managed by organized crime syndicates, which achieved new levels of power and unprecedented wealth from the bootlegging trade. Organized criminals were able to charge extremely high prices for alcohol because it was illegal, and they no doubt enjoyed this extra income.

By the end of the 1920s, which was a period of economic success that followed World War I and was called the Roaring Twenties, Prohibition was almost completely destroyed. In 1929, Mabel Walker Willebrandt, who was the assistant attorney general and fought to uphold Prohibition laws, openly admitted that huge quantities of illegal liquor were being consumed all across the country in rural hamlets and big cities alike, and the government was ineffective at stopping its sale.

The stock market crash of October 1929 and the Great Depression that followed brought the Prohibition era to a close. Americans of all political orientations argued that ending Prohibition would boost the struggling economy and help the government focus its energies on troubles that were directly affecting the lives of ordinary Americans. On December 5, 1933, another constitutional amendment—the 21st—was ratified by the required number of states, and it proclaimed that the 18th Amendment was no longer valid at a federal level. This marked the official end of Prohibition, and to date, the 18th Amendment is the only constitutional amendment to have been repealed after it was already ratified.

Though Prohibition was supported by the federal government, millions of Americans were still able to access alcohol by going to speakeasies, such as the one shown here.

Not Progressive Enough

Some Progressives tried to address the longstanding racial tensions in America. Instead of calling for equal rights for African Americans and other minority groups, though, Progressives turned to segregation as the best policy for reducing racial violence and defusing the racial divide that was shaking American society. For a political group that fought for better lives for many different social groups, it was a sign of the times that the Progressive movement did not fight against racial discrimination.

In the South, both formal laws, called Jim Crow laws, and unwritten rules denied African Americans access to many southern restaurants, hotels, theaters, pool halls, and swimming pools. Jim Crow laws also forced African Americans to accept inferior accommodations in public streetcars, theaters, schools, trains, and restrooms. In addition to this strict and dehumanizing segregation, the threat of racial violence hovered over every black family in the South. In fact, aggressive and hateful white-on-black violence was a daily reality of the Jim Crow South. Conditions in the North were better for African Americans, but only relative to the horrors of southern living. Residential segregation was commonplace in northern cities, and educational and employment opportunities in the North remained much better for whites than for blacks and most other minorities.

Despite a general disinterest in encouraging racial equality, Progressives did want to bring an end to the lynching and open terrorization of African Americans. They often genuinely wanted to help improve the lives of black people, but mostly agreed that the best way to accomplish this was to promote segregation. Few followers of the Progressive movement believed in the words of journalist William English Walling, who declared, "we must come to treat the negro [black man] on a plane of absolute political and social equality."[21] Most white Progressives believed, as did a huge number of other Americans, that whites were intellectually and morally superior to other races. This included leading reform voices, ranging from President Roosevelt to Protestant minister Josiah Strong, a founder of the Social Gospel movement. Their goal was to stabilize the uneasy race relations by reducing racial violence— not to lift African Americans to the same social and legal status as whites.

This attitude angered and frustrated early–20th century African American civil rights activists, such as W.E.B. DuBois and Monroe Trotter. They condemned segregation as a national moral outrage that discredited America's supposed ideals of democracy and fairness for all men and women. Even with the Civil War and the end of slavery more than 50 years before, racial prejudices were difficult to overcome. The three presidents of the Progressive Era decided that their chances of making other social, economic, and political improvements would be much better if they did not alienate southern lawmakers who vowed that they would fight to preserve segregation at all costs. As a result, segregation actually became even more firmly entrenched in American society during the first two decades of the 20th century.

The reformers made great strides in

other areas, such as cleansing political corruption, but they did not do enough to improve the lives of minority groups in America. Some historians have argued that their open support of segregationist practices was harmful to African Americans. This is now widely regarded as the most shameful chapter of the entire Progressive Era. "Segregation was ... a failure of imagination and nerve," one scholar concluded.

The rise of progressivism represented a remarkable reworking of middle-class ideology, a creative deployment of a [lot] of devices for reform, and a bold determination to take on some of the most basic and [difficult] issues of human existence. Willing to believe that a kind of "paradise" might really be attainable some day, progressives showed little fear in dealing with problems of gender, family, class, and economy—but not of race.[22]

Chapter Three

BIG BUSINESS AND LITTLE LABOR

Though the Progressive movement did little to fight for the equal rights of all races in America, they were able to achieve a number of important goals in other fields. Among their most prominent achievements was the reduction of exploitative practices of powerful corporate interests. For much of the mid-to-late 1800s, the businesses that gained extreme wealth due to the Industrial Revolution were able to do essentially whatever they wanted. This included bribing politicians, abusing workers, and manipulating prices. As soon as the Progressive Era began in the early 1900s, some of the worst of these issues started to fade.

Despite the tireless efforts of Progressive lawmakers and labor leaders, the life of the common, working-class family was still difficult in America's early 20th century. This is partially because government is simply unable to move quickly. Significant reforms took years to develop, and even more time to actually have an effect. Moreover, the split between politicians and activist groups was still powerful, despite a number of years of working together. The exploitation, corruption, and abuses of the 19th century still stuck out in the minds of civilian leaders. As a result, the Progressives were unable to form a long-lasting or powerful alliance with legislators, and though they still accomplished a great deal, their political power was somewhat limited.

Working Scared

In 1900, about 24 million people—roughly one-third of the nation's population of 76 million—made up the country's active workforce. The majority of these men, women, and children did jobs with their hands on docks, roads, and farms, or in factories, mines, and other people's houses. They practiced traditional crafts, such as tailoring and carpentry, in addition to newer arts, such as iron molding and metal cutting. They worked with huge machines in mills and factories and served as unskilled laborers in towns, farm hands in the countryside, cowboys on the range, and domestic servants in their own neighborhood. Nearly all of them—from the warehouse worker to the skilled carpenter—lived unstable, vulnerable lives, limited by low pay and a lack of opportunity. Unemployment, ill health, and premature death were menaces to everyone but the extremely wealthy.

Workers in manufacturing industries, for example, earned an average of only $3.80 per hour in 1909. Under this level of compensation, workers faced daily struggles to provide their families with decent shelter, clothing, and food. Laborers in the anthracite coal mining industry, one of the most dangerous industries in the nation, earned even less. The income of farmhands and other agricultural workers was among the lowest in the country, though they frequently received food and shelter as part of their compensation. Many unskilled and semiskilled workers also knew that their jobs could easily be lost at any time due to seasonal downturns, breakdowns of factory machinery, or shortages of the raw materials necessary for production.

Meanwhile, those who secured steady work, often faced the grim prospect of crippling injury or even death. Few jobs guaranteed safety for workers in the 20th century. "Every working-class occupation had its difficulties and dangers, from the explosions, fires, cave-ins, debilitating 'miner's lung,' and other notorious [dangers] of hard-rock mining in the West to the … asthma … tuberculosis, and maimings in the textile mills of the East."[23] In 1900 alone, 1,489 American coal miners lost their lives on the job. The American railroad industry, one of the biggest sectors of the economy at the turn of the century, experienced much higher death rates than that of other industrial countries, such as England.

The conditions in which American employees worked also took a tremendous toll on their morale. The men who fed coal to the roaring furnaces of the eastern steel foundries, slaughtered livestock in the filthy slaughterhouses of the Midwest, and hacked through the depths of the earth in search of western silver and copper went home dirty and exhausted every single day for years on end. Women and children were not spared, either. Millions suffered under grueling work conditions in steaming farm fields and on stifling factory floors. Women and children employed by textile manufacturing plants toiled six days a week, fourteen hours a day. According to one historian,

Their workplace was an overheated, poorly ventilated room that filled an entire floor … Screeching, clanking pulleys and levers and wheels roared with a deafening clatter; vibrations from the top-floor looms shook walls, ceilings, and floors as thousands of spring-loaded wood shuttles slammed

against the side frames of looms, then back across at lightning speeds; they rattled and hammered without pause. Even at a distance, several floors below in the spinning ... rooms, the mill girls lived with the explosive repetitive slap of those shuttles and the wheeze of whirring, straining metal wheels close by.[24]

Many workers in mining and other similar industries found themselves living in company towns. These were villages or towns in which most or all of the homes, stores, schools, hotels, hospitals, and other facilities were owned by a massively rich and powerful corporation. These towns were typically built up around the steel mill, mine, cannery, or factory, at which many of the residents worked for the company that owned the town. Many other municipalities, meanwhile, were not actually corporate-owned, but one employer provided so many jobs that its owners and managers were essentially the "bosses" of the entire town.

Some workers and their families favored the stability that some of these towns offered, but others hated working under the arrangement. They complained that it made them feel like medieval serfs, who were farmers who worked the land for a noble lord but did not profit. Some coal mining companies even compensated their workers

This picture shows an armed man standing guard over a company town in Alabama. The creation of company towns was just one of the abusive practices of powerful corporations in the 19th and 20th centuries.

Against Child Labor

In 1906, muckraker journalist John Spargo published *The Bitter Cry of the Children*, which documented the problem of child labor in America. Spargo's book described in cruel detail the lives of boys who worked in West Virginia's coal mines:

> The coal is hard, and accidents to the hands, such as cut, broken, or crushed fingers, are common among the boys. Sometimes there is a worse accident: a terrified shriek is heard, and a boy is mangled and torn in the machinery, or disappears in the chute to be picked out later smothered and dead. Clouds of dust fill the breakers [mining machines] and are inhaled by the boys, laying the foundations for asthma ... I once stood in a breaker for half an hour and tried to do the work a twelve-year-old boy was doing day after day, for ten hours at a stretch, for sixty cents a day. The gloom of the breaker appalled me. Outside the sun shone brightly ... and the birds sang in chorus with the trees and the rivers. Within the breaker there was blackness, clouds of deadly dust enfolded everything, the harsh, grinding roar of the machinery and the ceaseless rushing of coal through the chutes filled the ears ... I was covered from head to foot with coal dust, and for many hours afterwards I was [coughing up] some of the small particles of anthracite I had swallowed.[1]

1. John Spargo, *The Bitter Cry of the Children*. New York, NY: The Macmillan Company, 1906, pp. 164–165.

with special money that could only be used in the company's own store. To some, it felt alarmingly close to slavery. As one worker for the Pullman Palace Car Company stated, "We are born in a Pullman house. We are fed from a Pullman shop, taught in a Pullman school ... and when we die we shall be buried in a Pullman cemetery and go to a Pullman hell."[25]

Strength in Unions

It took until the turn of the 20th century for unions to be able to add their collective voice to the growing demand for major social and economic reforms. However, labor unions had actually been a fact of American life since the early 1800s. The first American unions were early tradesmen associations or guilds. These associations were made up of skilled craftsmen, and they played an important role in lifting the economic fortunes of carpenters, printers, machinists, glassmakers, and other workers with specialized skills. They set standards and helped keep employers—and employees—honest with one another.

As the Industrial Revolution swept the country in the 1850s and 1860s, however, the more modern forms of unions became prominent. In response to the increasingly abusive practices of big businesses, labor leaders began to bargain more aggressively on behalf of members with employers on a wide range of issues. These included wages, work hours, work rules, benefits, workplace safety, promotions, and other policies. By the 1850s, craftsmen's organizations, such as the International Typographical Union, had achieved nationwide reach. During the 1860s and 1870s, they managed to lift many of their members into the ranks of the American middle class. By the late 19th century, craft labor unions claimed hundreds of thousands of members—a significant portion of the American workforce. The largest of these union organizations was the national-level American Federation of Labor (AFL), an association that included 40 craft unions by 1892. It was founded in 1886 and headed by Samuel Gompers, who was originally the president of the cigar makers' union. The AFL had real political and economic influence.

The picture was far less optimistic, however, for most of America's unskilled and semiskilled laborers. The workers who toiled over the assembly lines of New England's textile plants or spent their days scouring coal, gold, or copper out of the mountains of the West had virtually no bargaining power with their corporate employers. They were at the mercy of the owners and managers of the great steel mills, mining companies, textile factories, and railroads of the industrial age. Most of these employers were willing to abuse and exploit their workers to produce higher profit margins. This led to larger paychecks for those at the top levels. This also kept wages low, and employees were forced to work at an exhausting pace and often in dangerous conditions. As one historical account noted, "[reckless] use of untested chemicals

The AFL distributed labels similar to this one all across America so people would know their purchases were going to support AFL unions.

The Courts Against the People

In the early 20th century, Progressives frequently criticized American judges for excessive interference in disputes between labor and management. Reformers and labor activists expressed particular outrage with the judges' frequent use of injunctions, or court orders, to cripple labor strikes and boycotts against corporations. "The results were devastating" for unions, one historian explained. "A judge could enjoin [command] thousands of workers at a time; he could tell them not to picket, not to march, not to meet, not to shout 'scab' at strikebreakers."[1]

The use of injunctions rose each decade from the 1880s through the 1920s, to the great disgust of labor leaders. John Mitchell, a labor activist associated with the United Mine Workers, wrote, "No weapon has been used with such disastrous effect against trade unions as the injunction in labor disputes ... It is difficult to speak in [calm] tone or moderate language of the savagery and venom with which unions have been [attacked] by the injunction."[2]

As frustration mounted, legislative allies of the labor movement vowed to disarm judges. However, most attempts to limit the ability of judges to get involved with management-labor lawsuits failed. This situation remained basically unchanged until 1932, when the Norris-LaGuardia Act was passed. This law placed significant new restrictions on judges' rights to impose injunctions in labor cases. It also guaranteed labor unions the right to meet and plan strikes, boycotts, and other protests without fear of retaliation.

1. Michael McGerr, *A Fierce Discontent: The Rise and Fall of the Progressive Movement in America*. New York, NY: Oxford University Press, 2005, p. 144.

2. Michael McGerr, *A Fierce Discontent*, p. 144.

and unregulated workplace environments gave rise to new deformities and illness. Each year, thousands were killed and maimed in America's notoriously unsafe work sites."[26]

Some unskilled workers looked to the craft unions for help, but the AFL and other established trade organizations showed little interest in lending a hand to factory workers, farming laborers, and other unskilled workers. "The skilled workers looked down on the unskilled, many of whom were recent immigrants, seeing them not as allies against management but as a burden, likely to bring down their own wages."[27] This understandably led to a division between labor forces—skilled and unskilled—that kept both sides relatively weak.

A few strong activists had managed to organize unions for unskilled workers, but these were mostly failures. The first national union created specifically to represent all types of workers—including the unskilled—was the National Labor Union, which was founded in 1866. It tried to go directly to lawmakers to improve working conditions, rather than relying on the employers themselves. It lasted just seven years until it collapsed under the strain of a national economic depression and a disastrous attempt by its leadership to form an independent political party.

A Time for Knights

The National Labor Union was succeeded by a far more successful organization named the Knights of Labor, which was founded in 1869 in Philadelphia. The Knights' platform, which called for an end to child labor, the institution of an eight-hour workday, and better wages, was enormously popular with the nation's factory workers. By 1886, the Knights had organized hundreds of successful strikes and expanded its membership to more than 700,000 workers— including women and African American workers, who were shut out by the AFL and other unions.

The success of the Knights of Labor turned out to be short-lived. Just after reaching its peak in 1886, it began to fall apart almost immediately. That year produced more than 1,000 strikes

nationwide in addition to the tragic Haymarket Riot, and public sympathy for aggressive unions began to fade. Moreover, they were doomed by bad strategic decisions, a prolonged economic depression, and growing public anxiety about violent protest. The AFL arose as the most prominent labor union in the 1890s, but around this same period, two other influential unions were founded. These organizations—the United Mine Workers of America (UMWA) and the Industrial Workers of the World (IWW)—also had an enormous impact on labor-management relations during the Progressive Era.

After it was created in 1890, the UMWA became the first successful industrial union of coal miners in American history. It struggled in its first years, as many unions do, but in the late 1890s and early 1900s, its president, John Mitchell, orchestrated several successful strikes against mine owners. These strikes led to sweeping reforms in mines all across the country.

The second major labor union to emerge at the dawn of the 20th century was the IWW (commonly known as "Wobblies"), founded in 1905 by representatives of more than 40 independent labor unions. The IWW never had a huge number of members, but the organization nevertheless had a huge impact on labor-management relations and American society.

A Radical Group

When the IWW was founded in 1905, it claimed that it would try to make a group

British Born, American Made

During his long service as the president of the American Federation of Labor, Samuel Gompers became one of the most influential labor leaders in U.S. history. Born on January 27, 1850, in London, Gompers immigrated to the United States from England with his family when he was 13 years old. He learned the cigar-making trade from his father, and in the 1870s, he became a leader of the Cigar Makers' International Union (CMIU).

In 1886, the CMIU united with several other trade unions to form the AFL. Gompers was the first president of the AFL, and with the exception of one year (1895), he headed the union until his death in 1924. Gompers focused on organizing trade workers with specialized knowledge and skills, rather than unskilled factory workers. This approach angered other labor activists, who accused Gompers of trying to create a class of workers who thought they were more important than common laborers. Regardless, Gompers's strategy was successful. Membership in the AFL was nearing 3 million by the time of his death on December 13, 1924.

Throughout his tenure, Gompers avoided the radical political activism and confrontational tactics that were the hallmarks of other unions. He focused on issues that were central to workers' lives, such as wages, workplace safety, and reasonable working hours. The labor agreements that he and the AFL negotiated helped many of its members gain greater economic and job security than American workers had ever enjoyed before.

Samuel Gompers spent a large portion of his life as the leader of the AFL. Under his direction, the labor organization grew to massive proportions and workers achieved new levels of benefits and fair treatment.

of "workers of this country into a working class movement that shall have for its purpose the emancipation [freedom] of the working class from the [slavery] of capitalism."[28] This attitude had come out of the brutal mining camps of the West, where IWW leaders "Big" Bill Haywood and Mary Harris "Mother" Jones had witnessed firsthand how mine owners used terror and violence to suppress union activities. In response, the IWW was fighting not only against abusive corporations, but also against the economic system of capitalism.

In the years following its founding, the Wobblies had a mixed influence on the Progressive Era. On the one hand, most Americans opposed their radical philosophy, which called for tearing down American society and building a new one that reflected the ideals of socialism or communism. Corporate interests took advantage of the American public's hostility to the IWW by repeatedly trying to link all labor activists and rebellious unions to the Wobblies. By doing this, they associated the relatively moderate reformers with the extremist ideas of the IWW. These efforts were effective, and they delayed some workplace reforms and encouraged a public distrust of unions.

The IWW also advanced the cause of the American worker in some ways. The organization's inclusion of women and African Americans was an important step in the development of the American labor movement. In addition, some other labor groups embraced the confrontational and aggressive tactics used by the Wobblies, and though they were frequently the subjects of intense scrutiny, IWW members were dedicated to their principles. This inspired other working men and women. Finally, the radicalism of the IWW and similar groups of that era convinced some of the most powerful people in America's corporate boardrooms and statehouses that some compromises simply had to be

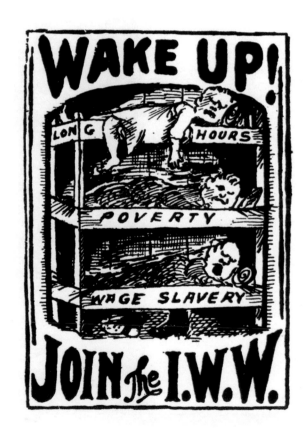

The IWW was an influential union in the early 20th century despite its radical and controversial goals and tactics.

made with the nation's angry industrial workers. Otherwise, they believed that a revolution, which the IWW campaigned for, might actually become a reality.

The dawning of the Progressive Era in the early decades of the 20th century brought big changes to the American labor movement. This time period was not without its disappointments for union activists and labor members. For instance, union membership did not increase very much from 1900 to 1915, and some of the labor movement's most prominent strikes and boycotts of these years did not end up making significant changes. Nonetheless, millions of working men and women across America earned substantially higher wages, worked fewer hours, and enjoyed a better quality of life than they had only a few short years before. Scholars credit many of these gains to the awkward, but effective, alliance that labor leaders forged with Progressive reformers.

Politics and Unions

Progressives were generally sympathetic to the struggles that working-class Americans faced in the new industrial age. As a result, they voiced support for the unionization of America and bargaining efforts of union organizations that focused on basic issues, such as higher pay and workplace safety. Middle-class reformers believed these improvements would reduce the growing class divisions that were causing so much discontent in American society and bring a greater measure of stability and peace to the nation as a whole.

Though many middle-class Progressives were supportive of moderate reform groups, most disliked and distrusted the more radical labor organizations, such as the IWW. They saw the IWW and other confrontational organizations as a threat to the stable, unified, and morally upright country that they were trying to build. The famous Progressive activist Jane Addams, for example, declared, "a moral revolution cannot be accomplished by men who are held together merely because they are all [hurt] under a sense of injury and injustice."[29]

Progressives also voiced frustration with some of the labor movement's policies and priorities. A large portion of unions, for example, restricted or banned women from membership. Even women who formed their own unions were not shielded from glaring gender discrimination. Because the AFL and other similar organizations were focused on improving the basic economic conditions of its members, they did not spend much effort on social or political issues, such as race and gender prejudice.

After the Women's Trade Union League was founded in 1903, it tried to associate itself with Gompers's powerful AFL and other major labor organizations. However, labor leadership all across America largely ignored the group and the issues it raised. Women activists who were fighting for what they called "bread and roses"—"bread" referring to basic economic needs and "roses" referring to dignity and hope for themselves

Progressive Governor, Senator, Hero

Robert M. La Follette served the people of Wisconsin in public office for most of his adult life. As governor of Wisconsin from 1901 to 1906, he helped many important business and political reforms see the light of day in his state. Thanks to La Follette's talents as a speaker and statesman, Wisconsin became a model of state government for Progressive leaders in other states. La Follette then moved on to Washington, D.C., where he served as a U.S. senator from 1906 until his death in 1925. During this period, he became known as one of the Senate's greatest champions of Progressive causes. In the following excerpt from his 1913 autobiography, La Follette explained what motivated him to pursue Progressive ideals throughout his career:

> If it can be shown that Wisconsin is a happier and better state to live in, that its institutions are more democratic, that the opportunities of all its people are more equal, that social justice more nearly prevails, that human life is safer and sweeter—then I shall rest content in the feeling that the Progressive movement has been successful. And I believe all these things can really be shown, and that there is no reason now why the movement should not expand until it covers the entire nation. While much has been accomplished, there is still a world of problems yet to be solved; we have just begun; there is hard fighting, and a chance for the highest patriotism, still ahead of us. The fundamental problem as to which shall rule, men or property, is still unsettled; it will require the highest qualities of heroism, the profoundest devotion to duty in this and in the coming generation, to reconstruct our institutions to meet the requirements of a new age. May such brave and true leaders develop that the people will not be led astray.[1]

1. Robert M. La Follette, *La Follette's Autobiography: A Personal Narrative of Political Experience*. Madison, WI: University of Wisconsin Press, 2013, pp. 157–158.

and their children—were outraged at this condescending and unfriendly attitude. This attitude hurt the labor cause within the larger Progressive movement. Many Progressives were women who supported suffrage, and many male Progressives also supported increased women's rights, including the right to vote. To these

Americans, the behavior of the AFL and other male-dominated unions toward women was insulting and unfair.

Even so, Progressives and mainstream labor groups were able to find common ground in many other areas. Both movements fought hard to reduce child labor in America, and they supported each other's efforts to pass new laws protecting women in the workplace. However, the motivations that drove these groups to unite were somewhat different. Progressives crusaded against corporate exploitation of women and children on the grounds that they were immoral and cruel. Labor unions also saw these corporate abuses as inhumane, and they battled them for that reason, but they also wanted to pass business reform laws in these areas because they knew that such laws would increase the demand for adult male workers. This would give unions more bargaining power, leading to even higher wages and quality of life improvements. A similar attitude drove labor leaders to support new immigration restrictions that were passed during the early 1900s.

Getting More Involved

Progressive efforts to restrict corporate exploitation of workers were driven by the widespread perception that the extremely wealthy businessmen—not lawmakers or the people they supposedly represented—had become the people in charge of making American society. The primary weapon that Progressives used against corporations was a sweeping new set of governmental regulations. These regulations helped municipal, state, and local governments control corporate behavior, but they were not imposed without a fight from the powerful corporations that had called the shots in America for so many years.

Reformers recognized that these companies were formidable foes. Corporations benefited from cheap labor, territorial expansion, new energy resources, and an almost complete lack of laws governing business behavior. Companies and huge trusts grew into economic giants during the Industrial Revolution. By the Gilded Age, the use of mergers and acquisitions of competitors to create powerful corporate giants had reached staggering levels. Between 1897 and 1904, 4,227 firms were merged to form just 257 corporations. The largest of these mergers was the 1901 creation of the U.S. Steel Corporation. This new massive corporation, organized by famous financier J.P. Morgan, was worth $1.4 billion ($40 billion today) and controlled a majority of the nation's steel production immediately. By 1904, roughly 40 percent of the nation's total manufacturing output was controlled by just 318 companies.

At the dawn of the 20th century, the United States government had little legal power to slow the growing concentration of wealth and economic power in the hands of these powerful and influential corporate machines. Big businesses were experienced at using their influence to destroy any business regulations before state legislatures or Congress

Presidential Progress

In 1910, President Theodore Roosevelt delivered what became known as his "New Nationalism" speech. This powerful speech included many of Roosevelt's Progressive political beliefs, and it turned out to be an early sign that Roosevelt was planning to run for president again in 1912 (eventually losing to Woodrow Wilson). He explicitly discussed the corrupting influence that large and powerful businesses were having on the supposedly pure United States government:

> I stand for the square [fair] deal. But when I say that I am for the square deal, I mean not merely that I stand for fair play under the present rules of the game, but that I stand for having those rules changed so as to work for a more substantial equality of opportunity and of reward for equally good service ... Now, this means that our government, national and State, must be freed from the sinister influence or control of special interests. Exactly as the special interests of cotton and slavery threatened our political integrity before the Civil War, so now the great special business interests too often control and corrupt the men and methods of government for their own profit. We must drive the special interests out of politics ... There can be no effective control of corporation while their political activity remains. To put an end to it will be neither a short nor an easy task, but it can be done.[1]

One of the greatest defenders of Progressive beliefs was Theodore Roosevelt. He was not afraid to dissolve trusts and regulate corporate greed.

1. Richard D. Heffner and Alexander Heffner, *A Documentary History of the United States: Expanded and Updated Ninth Edition*. New York, NY: Signet, 2013.

could pass them. Even when reformers did manage to pass laws restricting corporate monopolies or regulating corporate activities, the business-friendly U.S. courts often ripped the laws to shreds or rendered them useless.

Taking It to Court

Many reform efforts were actually rejected, manipulated, or weakened by an American court system that remained firmly in favor of corporations on most matters of law. Many judges believed in a laissez-faire (from the French for "let people do what they want") economic philosophy. According to this philosophy, government had no right to interfere with private business activity. Instead, it should let the free market operate without restrictions, because restrictions would eventually smother economic growth and ultimately victimize all members of society. "[Selected] mostly from the upper class, justices [judges] naturally defended the interests of property against labor," one scholar explained. "Moreover, courts rightly saw working-class mutualism [working together] as a threat to their authority and to the individualist values embedded in the American common law."[30]

This attitude extended all the way up to the nine justices of the U.S. Supreme Court. In the landmark 1905 case *Lochner v. New York*, the justices struck down, by a narrow margin of 5–4, a New York State law that limited the number of hours that bakery employees could work. "Statutes [laws] of the nature of that under review,"

one of the justices wrote, "limiting the hours in which grown and intelligent men may labor to earn their living, are mere meddlesome interferences with the rights of the individual."[31]

This ruling, which ignored the fact that bakery workers faced extreme pressure to work long hours, often early in the morning and late at night, or risk being fired, ushered in the so-called "Lochner era" in American legal history. During this time period, which extended into the mid-1930s, the Supreme Court struck down or limited a number of Progressive government regulations that had been created to give new economic and workplace protections to American workers. In most cases, the Court stated that these new laws and regulations were unconstitutional.

Responding to Tragedies

Faced with such clear hostility to their efforts, some reformers wondered if they would ever be successful in their efforts to place limits on the nation's corporate giants. Over time, however, Progressives who were intent on imposing meaningful corporate reforms and improving the lives of workers fought through the setbacks and made at least some steady progress. Some infamous tragedies of American business history, such as the Triangle Shirtwaist Factory fire and the Ludlow Massacre, were important milestones in this campaign.

The Triangle Shirtwaist Factory fire occurred on March 25, 1911, at a textile sweatshop in New York City. It

This image shows the aftermath of the brutal response to the Ludlow workers' strike in 1914.

was reportedly caused by an employee discarding a still-lit cigarette indoors. It began on the eighth floor of the building, which was too high for fire rescue ladders to reach. Moreover, the outdoor fire escapes had collapsed due to the weight of so many panicking people, and some of the sweatshop's doors had been locked. Many employees found themselves trapped. By the time the flames had been extinguished, 129 women and 17 men, mostly immigrant workers, had been killed.

The Ludlow Massacre occurred in 1914. In this incident, Colorado National Guard troops had been sent to keep the peace between 10,000 striking miners and their employer, the Colorado Fuel and Iron Company. The strike had been going on since September 1913, and there was violence between the workers and the National Guard troops because the soldiers acted in favor of the company. On April 19, 1914, the National Guardsmen opened fire on the strikers' encampment, and the workers fought back. The violence lasted for the entire day, during which 2 women and 11 children in the miners' camp were killed. In total, 22 workers and 3 National Guardsmen lost their lives. In the aftermath of the massacre, the famous labor organizer Mary Harris "Mother" Jones declared,

What does all this [conflict] growing out of the coal strike and the Ludlow Massacre mean? It means that the workers would rather die fighting to

protect their women and children than to die in death-trap mines producing more wealth for the Rockefellers to use in crushing their children ... It means that the whole nation is on the verge of a revolution.[32]

To many union members and other working-class Americans, these events showed just how helpless they were in the face of corporate ruthlessness. However, tragedies such as the Triangle fire and the deaths in Ludlow actually generated important public and political support for meaningful business reforms and the wider Progressive cause. In the wake of the Triangle deaths, the state of New York created a Factory Investigating Commission, which eventually passed more than 30 new safety regulations for factories all across the state. Over the next several years, these laws became the inspiration for dozens of safety regulations in other states, and they influenced the future of labor laws in America.

The events in Ludlow did not produce any substantial legislation to protect future strikers. Congress held a series of investigative hearings, but no significant changes were made. The massacre did, however, increase membership in the UMWA by 4,000. This helped strengthen the UMWA, which became one of the most influential mining unions in the country. A more powerful union would eventually be able to pressure lawmakers at the national level.

The strengthening public support for Progressive reform was the single most important factor in finally breaking down the walls that huge businesses had built to preserve their wealthy empires. This support, which was nurtured by muckraker journalists and eloquent activists and heightened by events such as the Triangle Shirtwaist Factory tragedy, became particularly strong in middle-class communities. As union numbers swelled and the middle class began calling for reform, legislators were faced with a choice: pass Progressive laws or lose their office.

Many politicians—from the city level to the federal government—chose to side with big business. As a result, in the 1890s and early 1900s, Progressives were elected to serve as mayors, state legislators, and U.S. congressmen in greater numbers than ever before. Reformers such as Hazen S. Pingree (mayor of Detroit), Tom Johnson (mayor of Cleveland), Albert B. Cummins (governor and U.S. senator for Iowa), Robert M. La Follette (governor and U.S. senator for Wisconsin), and Theodore Roosevelt (governor of New York and president of the United States) effectively championed Progressive solutions to the wide variety of social, political, and economic problems troubling the nation. The biggest Progressive political event of the 20th century was the start of Roosevelt's presidency of the United States on September 14, 1901. When Roosevelt became president, a bold new age of corporate reform and government regulation began in America.

Chapter Four

PRESIDENTIAL POLICIES

In the final years of the 19th century, the Progressive movement was starting to grow powerful and influential all across the United States. Millions of Americans were tired of the way their working-class neighbors were treated by the country's newly made corporate giants. Child labor was still a plague, workplace safety was nonexistent, and lawmakers were slow to regulate powerful business interests. Some improvements had been made, but the Progressive movement did not reach the status of political heavyweight until 1901—when Theodore Roosevelt ascended to the presidency after the assassination of William McKinley. A strong, heroic, and outspoken supporter of Progressive ideals, Roosevelt was the perfect man to make sweeping, permanent changes to American industry. He became a symbol for the strength, justice, and morality that the Progressives wanted to achieve in the United States.

Inspired and influenced by Roosevelt's eight-year term, the next two presidents, William Howard Taft and Woodrow Wilson, kept up some of the Progressive movement's momentum. Elected in 1908, Taft followed in some of his predecessor's footsteps by carrying on some of Roosevelt's policies. However, though Progressives had high hopes for Taft's term, he did not make as much of an effort as they wanted. He lacked the compelling leadership ability of Roosevelt, and his political philosophy was simply not as progressive. In 1912, he was replaced by Wilson. A member of the opposite party (Roosevelt and Taft were Republicans; Wilson was a Democrat.), he nevertheless continued to encourage improvements for the lives of millions of working-class Americans. These three men were the presidents that ruled over the Progressive Era.

Transformative Years

Roosevelt was born in New York City on October 27, 1858, to a prosperous family. He was intelligent and curious, but also small and sickly; his parents worried that he was destined for a short life. Even at a young age, however, Roosevelt displayed a high level of fortitude and determination. He took up boxing and weightlifting to improve his health and spent countless hours hunting, camping, and otherwise exploring the outdoors. By the time he graduated from Harvard University in 1880, he was a tough, strong young man. His love of the outdoors, nature, and tests of physical strength continued well into his adult life.

Roosevelt's career in politics began modestly with a two-year stint as a New York state assemblyman from 1882 to 1884. In February 1884, his wife of four years, Alice Hathaway Lee, died after giving birth to their daughter, also named Alice. The grieving Roosevelt spent the next two years in the Dakota Territory, where he worked as a cattle rancher. He quickly developed a reputation throughout the territory for his natural leadership capabilities and his fierce style of patriotism. In 1886, he married Edith Kermit Carow, with whom he eventually had four sons and one daughter.

Even at this early stage in his life, Roosevelt exhibited a strong Progressive mindset. On July 4, 1886, for example, he electrified an audience of western farmers and ranchers with an Independence Day speech that blended

After surviving a sickly childhood, Theodore Roosevelt tried to build up his physical strength by spending time outdoors. He retained this love of nature forever.

patriotic pride with an unmistakable hostility toward the greed of the nation's corrupt corporate figures. "Like all Americans, I like big things," he declared:

> [B]ig prairies, big forests and mountains, big wheat fields, railroads—and herds of cattle, too—big factories, steamboats, and everything else. But we must keep steadily in mind that no people were ever yet benefited by riches if their prosperity corrupted their virtue. It is of more importance that we should show ourselves honest, brave, truthful, and intelligent, than that we should own all the railways and grain elevators in the world. We have fallen heirs to the most glorious heritage a people ever received, and each one must do his part if we wish to show that the nation is worthy of its good fortune.[33]

In 1889, Roosevelt returned east to accept a position as a member of the U.S. Civil Service Commission. Over the next six years, the reform-minded Republican became known for his crusades against political corruption in New York City, and he was appointed to a position as president of the New York City Board of Police Commissioners. He battled corrupt elements in the police force and continued building his reputation as a strictly principled public official by enforcing unpopular laws banning the sale of alcohol on Sundays. "I do not deal with public sentiment,"

he declared. "I deal with the law."[34]

In 1897, Roosevelt moved on to the position of assistant secretary of the navy. In May 1898, he resigned this powerful office so he could personally fight in the Spanish-American War. He joined as second in command of the First Volunteer Cavalry regiment, which was popularly known as the "Rough Riders." That unit's actions were widely publicized during the war, and Roosevelt's outstanding heroism and fierce battle instincts made him a military hero by the time he returned to the United States several months later. Roosevelt then capitalized on his fame and his popularity with reformers across the state to win the governorship of New York in the 1898 election. He served as governor for only two years, but during that time, he passed numerous state laws against child labor, abusive treatment of workers, and other causes that were important to American Progressives.

In 1900, Roosevelt was asked to run for vice president on the re-election ticket of President William McKinley. (McKinley's previous vice president, Garret Hobart, died in office in November 1899.) Roosevelt accepted the offer, and he spent the fall delivering spirited campaign speeches across the country. The McKinley-Roosevelt ticket won the 1900 presidential election by a comfortable margin over the Democratic ticket of William Jennings Bryan and Adlai E. Stevenson. Ten months later, tragedy struck the country when President McKinley was assassinated

President William McKinley was popular before he was assassinated in 1901. His successor went on to be one of the most accomplished presidents in history.

than the voters' ballot—Roosevelt was not afraid to immediately start ruling with his trademark blend of ferocious determination, vigorous energy, and unshakable self-confidence.

Roosevelt also quickly notified everyone in the federal government that he did not feel any obligation to blindly follow the pro-business policies of McKinley or other Republican legislators. Only four months after being sworn in, Roosevelt delivered a rousing speech to Congress. He informed his listeners that he intended to tame the corporate trusts that dominated America in the 1890s and early 1900s. He also showed, however, that he would not blindly follow Progressive leaders, either:

by a gunman in Buffalo, New York. He died on September 14, 1901, roughly one week after the attack. Roosevelt was immediately sworn in as America's 26th president.

White House Changes

When Roosevelt assumed the presidency, he became the youngest president in the nation's history to that point. Despite his relative youth—and the fact that he had reached the position as a result of an assassin rather

The captains of industry who have driven the railway systems across this continent, who have built up our commerce, who have developed our manufactures, have on the whole done great good to our people. Without them the material development of which we are so justly proud could never have taken place ... Yet it is also true that there are real and grave evils ... and a resolute and practical effort must be made to correct these evils.

A Difficult Relationship

Although he was extremely supportive of many Progressive reforms, President Theodore Roosevelt disliked Upton Sinclair and the other crusading journalists who published similar books and articles. He thought that they painted an unfair picture of American business and society, and he complained that their reports increased public support for radical and irresponsible "solutions" to America's ills. He also criticized some of these muckraker journalists for reporting things that may not be factually accurate.

In an April 14, 1906, speech, Roosevelt coined the term "muckraker" to describe these journalists. Today, the term is used to describe investigative reporters who are not afraid to write stories that expose problems with powerful interests. When Roosevelt used the term, however, it was an insult based on a character in John Bunyan's novel *Pilgrim's Progress*. This character never looked away from evil to admire the good in the world:

> Now, it is very necessary that we should not flinch from seeing what is vile and debasing. There is filth on the floor, and it must be scraped up with the muckrake; and there are times and places where this service is the most needed of all the services that can be performed. But the man who never does anything else, who never thinks or speaks or writes, save of his feats with the muck-rake, speedily becomes, not a help to society ... but one of the most potent forces for evil ... There should be relentless exposure of an attack upon every evil man whether politician or business man, [and] every evil practice, whether in politics, in business, or in social life. I [encourage] every writer or speaker ... provided always that he ... is of use only if [he] is absolutely truthful.[1]

1. Quoted in Michael Waldman, *My Fellow Americans: The Most Important Speeches of America's Presidents, From George Washington to Barack Obama*. Naperville, IL: Sourcebooks, 2003, p. 65.

There is a widespread conviction in the minds of the American people that the great corporations ... are [sometimes] hurtful to the general welfare ... in my judgment this conviction is right.[35]

Roosevelt's first big battles against the nation's corporate powers came quickly. In early 1902, the powerful financiers J.P. Morgan and John D. Rockefeller maneuvered to combine a series of railroad lines into the Northern Securities Company. This merger would have given these men and their business allies a profitable stranglehold over rail transport between Chicago and the West Coast. When Roosevelt heard about the scheme, though, he used the antitrust restrictions of the almost forgotten Sherman Act to block it. Because the Sherman Act had rarely been used to actually prevent large trusts from forming, Morgan and Rockefeller were stunned. They frantically tried to convince Roosevelt to let the deal go through. Roosevelt flatly refused on the grounds that the deal would give Morgan and his partners an unfair business monopoly. Morgan responded by unleashing his corporate attorneys on the administration, and the case reached the Supreme Court. In a landmark 1904 decision, the Supreme Court sided with Roosevelt, and the trust was busted.

Roosevelt also became engaged in an even more famous fight with powerful corporate interests. In May 1902, more than 147,000 members of the UMWA called a strike against mine owners in Pennsylvania, home of the nation's largest anthracite coal mines. Weary of working exhausting hours in dangerous mines for insultingly low wages, the strikers demanded corporate recognition of the UMWA, higher pay, and other concessions. The mine owners responded with contempt, refusing all requests to even meet with UMWA representatives to discuss a solution.

Roosevelt monitored the situation quietly for several months, but the threat of winter coal shortages to thousands of Americans on the East

The coal mines of Pennsylvania employed young boys at the start of the 20th century. Part of the motivation for the 1902 strikes was to get better conditions for all the workers.

Coast eventually forced him to act. In October, he organized and supervised a conference between UMWA president John Mitchell and the mine owners. The disrespectful attitude of the mine owners angered Roosevelt so much that he announced that he would use federal troops to seize the mines and operate them until the mine owners agreed to arbitration to settle the strike. This stunning threat convinced management to agree to make some concessions. A few months later, the labor-management dispute was solved when the company granted the miners a wage increase and agreed to several other union demands. Even more important, Roosevelt's stand with the miners had great symbolic value. "The federal government, for the first time in its history, had intervened in a strike not to break it, but to bring about a peaceful settlement. The great anthracite strike of 1902 cast a long shadow."[36]

Forcing a New Era

As the 1904 presidential election approached, Roosevelt was confident that he would be remaining in the White House for at least four more years. For one thing, most Americans enjoyed his vigorous, confident personality. He was a natural leader. Author Edith Wharton commented, "He was so alive at all points, and so gifted with the rare [ability] of living intensely and entirely in every moment as it passed, that each of those encounters [with Roosevelt] glows in me."[37] Americans also respected Roosevelt's exploits as a hunter, outdoorsman, and soldier, and they admired his sharp and restless intellect. As one biographer wrote,

The President is … capable of [explaining] German poetry to Lutheran preachers, and comparing recently [discovered] Gaelic letters with Hopi Indian lyrics. He is recognized as the world authority on big American game mammals, and is an ornithologist [bird scientist] of some note … Roosevelt is equally at home with experts in naval strategy, forestry, Greek drama, cowpunching, metaphysics, protective coloration, and football techniques.[38]

Finally, Roosevelt had the support of the large American middle class, which had become firmly Progressive by the opening years of the 20th century. "Progressives believed that government at every level—local, state, and federal—had to be enrolled in the fight [for fairness and democracy] through the direct participation of the people," one historian wrote. "Legislation was necessary to protect woman and child workers, to clean up slums, improve housing, and control … corporations, but first government itself had to be reformed. And to do that it was necessary to rescue the democratic process from [businesses] whose only concern was in increasing their power and profits."[39] During Roosevelt's first three years in office, Progressive-minded Americans had become convinced that he was the right man to implement such reforms.

Roosevelt highlighted his reputation as a bold reformer throughout the 1904 election campaign. He promised a "Square Deal" administration, in which no interest group would receive better treatment over another. His words triggered resistance from pro-business Republicans who disliked Roosevelt's trust-busting policies. These politicians generally stayed quiet, however, because they feared the prospect of a Populist Democratic administration even more.

As predicted, Roosevelt remained in the White House, winning about 56 percent of the popular vote against Democratic nominee Alton B. Parker (38 percent) and Socialist candidate Eugene V. Debs (3 percent). Roosevelt accurately interpreted the election results as a confirmation that Americans favored his Progressive policies, and he spent the next four years in the White House fighting for one bold initiative after another.

Making Moderate Waves

During his second term in office, Roosevelt prosecuted more than 40 antitrust cases against corporate giants, pushed the United States into a much more prominent role in international affairs, and changed the government's role in American society. Despite all this, few of Roosevelt's Progressive ideals and policies were truly radical. He was a strong political moderate who firmly believed in and supported both businesses, as long as they were ethical and fair, and the rights of the working class, as long

as they did not want to slow down the growth of the economy. In fact, one of his more powerful motivations for challenging powerful corporations, battling political corruption, and addressing social problems was to keep the radical forces in American society—extremely pro-business Conservatives on one side and Socialists and Communists on the other—from gaining influence.

During his last years in the White House, Roosevelt openly complained about some of the Progressive activists and journalists who spoke out against political and corporate corruption. He believed that even some of the most prominent reformers were fools who were not respected by working-class Americans. "They had not the slightest understanding of the needs, interests, ways of thought, and convictions of the average small man; and the small man felt this ... and sensed that they were really not concerned with his welfare,"[40] Roosevelt claimed.

Though he spoke out against obvious corporate abuses, Roosevelt also believed that an un-American feeling of envy was present in some criticisms of the wealthy and powerful. He argued that some Progressives were automatically—and unfairly—biased against anyone wealthy, even if they were running a fair and honest business. "The unscrupulous rich man who seeks to exploit and oppress those who are less well off is ... identical with, the unscrupulous poor man who desires to [steal from] and oppress those who are better off,"[41] he once said. On another

A Better System?

As the Progressive movement gained strength in America during the end of the 19th century and the first two decades of the 20th century, many large companies turned to systems that were termed welfare capitalism. Under these plans, companies invested large sums of money in social and education programs for their employees. Industrial giants, such as U.S. Steel, General Electric, Ford Motor Company, International Harvester, National Cash Register, and H.J. Heinz, paid for company baseball teams, gardening clubs, marching bands, swimming pools, nursing clinics, cooking classes, citizenship classes, and other perks. Some companies even offered profit sharing and private retirement plans for employees who qualified (generally a small percentage of the overall work force). The goal of these programs was to improve the image of American business—to prove that industrial giants were capable of taking care of their employees.

Management commonly characterized these programs as examples of their respect and appreciation for their employees. Union leaders and business reformers did not view these programs in a favorable light. They aggressively criticized them, arguing that welfare capitalism was nothing more than bribery intended to keep employees from supporting or joining unions. According to these critics, corporations had figured out that it was cheaper for them to pay for baseball uniforms, gardens, and sewing classes than it was for them to agree to the wage increases or shorter work weeks that unions demanded.

occasion, he openly acknowledged that America was "passing through a period of great unrest—social, political, and industrial unrest." He continued to warn:

[As long] as this [unrest] throughout the country takes the form of a fierce discontent with evil, of a determination to punish the [creators] of evil, whether in industry or politics, the feeling is to be … welcomed as a sign of healthy life.

If, on the other hand, it turns into a mere crusade of appetite against appetite, of a contest between the brutal greed of the "have-nots" and the brutal greed of the "haves," then it has no significance for good, but only for evil.[42]

Permanent Changes

These concerns, however, did not prevent Roosevelt from remodeling the guiding philosophy of American government during his second term in office. He believed that the role of government in American society had to be expanded in order for the nation to adapt to the huge cultural and economic changes brought about by the Industrial Revolution. He was convinced that the future of the country would be lost if he could not restore public faith in the basic principles of justice and democracy upon which the United States had been founded.

This belief drove Roosevelt's decision to support a wide range of new business regulations during his second term. He persuaded Congress to create a bureau of corporations to investigate and regulate big business. He also used his incredible ability as a public speaker to generate widespread support for numerous laws that were designed to improve workplace safety, stop child labor, punish slumlords, weed out political corruption, and help small business owners.

One of Roosevelt's greatest triumphs was the strengthening of the Interstate Commerce Commission (ICC), which had been founded in 1887 to regulate railroads. Until Roosevelt signed the Hepburn Act in 1906, however, it was largely ineffective. The Hepburn Act empowered the ICC to set reasonable railroad rates for passenger travel and shipping and prosecute companies that engaged in unethical business practices. The revolutionary law also required that railroad companies prepare an annual report on their business, which the ICC would investigate. This helped prevent corruption and abuses and exponentially increased the effectiveness of the ICC.

Formed in 1887, the Interstate Commerce Commission did not actually get the real power to enforce its guidelines until the 1906 Hepburn Act.

From President to President

Woodrow Wilson, who served as the 28th president of the United States from 1913 to 1921, was born on December 28, 1856, in Staunton, Virginia. The son of a Presbyterian minister, he grew up in Georgia, North Carolina, and South Carolina. In 1875, he moved to the East Coast to attend Princeton University in New Jersey. He always regarded himself as a southerner,

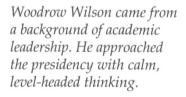

Woodrow Wilson came from a background of academic leadership. He approached the presidency with calm, level-headed thinking.

Roosevelt also defied powerful corporate interests by protecting immense tracts of American wilderness from exploitative logging, mining, and other development. During its first 125 years of existence, the United States had set aside very little of its land for conservation purposes. In fact, territorial, state, and federal government leaders had let corporations do whatever they wanted to the nation's forests, rivers, and mineral resources for generations. Roosevelt set a dramatic new course in America's treatment of its abundant—but not inexhaustible—natural resources. Today, he is famous as being one of the fathers of American conservation efforts.

By the time Roosevelt left the White House in 1909, he had added almost

though, and he attended law school at the University of Virginia.

After earning his Ph.D., Wilson was named president of Princeton University in 1902. He served in that position for eight years. In 1910, he won the governorship of New Jersey as a Democrat. During this period, Wilson's calm, quiet manner and his past career in higher education prompted some journalists to call him the "schoolmaster in politics." His Progressive ideals made him popular with the state's citizens, and Democratic Party leaders were quickly convinced that he was an attractive presidential candidate.

Wilson won the party's presidential nomination in 1912 and won the election by a wide margin, partially because Republicans split their vote between candidate William Taft and Theodore Roosevelt, who waged an independent campaign. Wilson also easily won again in 1916. During Wilson's two terms, he advanced the Progressive agenda in many areas and successfully guided the nation through World War I. After the war, however, his efforts to create an international organization of governments working together, called the League of Nations, proved unpopular with many Americans. He also retreated from the Progressive policies that made him popular after the public began resisting them.

230 million acres (93 million ha) to the nation's protected natural areas. Using this land, he founded dozens of wildlife refuges, established a series of national monuments, created new national parks, and protected new national forests. Some of these areas, such as national forests, continued to be utilized commercially, but the Roosevelt administration passed laws and established agencies to ensure that these resources would be used more responsibly. This ensured that the country's natural resources would be passed along to future generations. One biographer wrote that Roosevelt "was able to merge his love of nature and its beauty with his protective instincts, to offer it as a gift to all Americans [forever]. Little or,

perhaps, nothing else gave him more satisfaction as a public servant."[43]

In a broader sense, Roosevelt's eight years in office changed the way Americans thought about the role of government in their lives. He had also given the Progressive movement many of its greatest triumphs. His successors—first William Howard Taft and then Woodrow Wilson—would build on his record of Progressivism, but neither man would capture the hearts of Progressives in the way that Roosevelt did during his years in the White House. He was a strong, charismatic, and revolutionary leader.

A Decade of Changes

Following Roosevelt, many business regulations became a reality during the administrations of presidents William Howard Taft and Woodrow Wilson. Both Taft and Wilson recognized the continued public demand for increased government supervision of corporate behavior and economic activity, and many of their business policies reflected this reformist spirit. "We have come upon a very different age from any that preceded us," Woodrow Wilson said during a campaign speech.

There is a sense in which in our day the individual has been submerged. In most parts of the country men work, not for themselves, not as partners in the old way in which they used to work, but generally as employees— in a higher or lower grade—of great corporations. There was a time when corporations played a very minor part in our business affairs, but now they play the chief part, and most men are the servants of the corporations.[44]

The Taft administration enjoyed several major victories in its efforts to restore greater balance to the relationship between American corporations and their employees and customers. Taft supported the Mann-Elkins Act of 1910, an important law that brought the nation's powerful telephone, telegraph, and cable industries under increased government regulation. He also carried on Roosevelt's legacy of trust-busting. His administration broke up numerous corporate trusts, including Standard Oil, which was the largest company in American history until the Supreme Court ordered its dissolution in 1911.

Taft also advocated for two important pieces of antitrust legislation that eventually became law during Wilson's presidency. The first of these, the Federal Trade Commission Act, was passed in September 1914. It established the Federal Trade Commission (FTC) and gave it powers to eliminate and prevent business monopolies in all industries. The FTC was also given authority to ensure fair business competition among corporations of all shapes and sizes.

President Wilson also signed the second of these acts, the Clayton Antitrust Act, into law in 1914. This legislation was essentially a much tougher version of the 1890 Sherman Antitrust Act. It outlawed certain mergers and a variety of unfair business practices, including exclusive sales contracts, local price-cutting designed to bankrupt smaller competitors, and rebates. The Clayton Act also formally legalized peaceful labor actions, such as strikes, boycotts, and picketing, and it placed the nation's first restrictions on judges' use of injunctions against labor activity. It was a significant victory for the Progressive movement.

By the time America entered World War I in 1917, these acts—combined with a number of more specific laws, such as the 1916 Adamson Act, which mandated an eight-hour workday for railroad employees—had ushered in a new age of government regulation over the affairs of business and commerce. Though some conservative critics spoke against these changes, millions of Americans were beginning to see their lives improve substantially.

NO END TO PROGRESS

When Woodrow Wilson won the 1912 election, the Progressive Era was near its peak. All across America, there was a nearly unanimous call for an increase in fair business practices, protection for workers, and a return to a pure, uncorrupted America. William Howard Taft's term as president did not produce immediately substantial changes, so the American people voted in Woodrow Wilson. For most of Wilson's first term, he was popular and supported new laws and regulations that improved peoples' lives. To many Americans, it seemed like the Progressive movement was going to be in force forever.

However, before the end of the 1920s, the Progressives had all but disappeared, and the Age of Reform came crashing down. The reason for this abrupt destruction was simple: World War I. After America entered the largest and most deadly war the world had ever seen, there was a powerful backlash against the Progressive movement. The end of the Great War, as it was sometimes called, brought unprecedented wealth to America, and it emerged as a major player in world affairs. The heavily regulated Progressive Era was now seen as a mistake, as more and more people began believing in the power of the free market and the individual. Despite the collapse of the Progressive movement, however, the United States has still been progressing—socially, politically, and economically—for the past century.

A World War

The United States was not the only country that had been dramatically changed by the Industrial Revolution. The nations of Europe had also experienced great economic growth and social turmoil. By the early 20th century, the continent had become an unstable land filled with social upheaval, shifting military alliances, and ambition for greater wealth and power.

The event that ignited all of these volatile elements was the assassination of Archduke Franz Ferdinand of Austria-Hungary on June 28, 1914. Ferdinand was killed by a fanatic from Serbia, a country next to Austria. The two nations had been experiencing tense relations in the years leading up to the assassination. Austria-Hungary's desire to punish Serbia for this shocking murder was supported by Germany, which was ruled by an ambitious military government that had amassed the largest army in the world.

During the next few weeks, political leaders in Europe showed little interest in avoiding war. Instead, patriotic pride, the desire to seize new territory and power, and longstanding prejudices against other nationalities drove all these nations to mobilize their armies against one another. By August, Europe had divided into two camps— the Allies (led by Russia, France, and England) and the Central Powers (led by Germany, Turkey, and Austria-Hungary)—and entered into World War I.

For the next three years, the warring armies attacked each other and the cities of Europe with brutal force. The conflict marked the first widespread use of chemical weapons, the first mass bombardment of civilians by airplane, and

After years of political tension in Europe, the assassination of Archduke Franz Ferdinand was enough to set off a massive global conflict.

the first widespread use of a rapid-fire machine gun. This same time period also witnessed the first genocide of the 20th century, when more than 1 million ethnic Armenians perished at the hands of Turkey's government. By the war's end, roughly 8.5 million soldiers and as many as 13 million civilians were dead.

The Great War was locked in a stalemate until 1917. Neither side could make considerable gains, and soldiers were dying in failed attempts to take territories. This changed when the United States entered the conflict in support of the Allies. President Woodrow Wilson, who tried to hold off entry into the war for as long as possible, was forced to mobilize the armed forces after Central Powers ships attacked and sank a series of merchant ships with ties to the United States. He recalibrated the nation's government and its massive industrial resources so that it could participate in the war effort. By early 1918, it was clear that the economic, industrial, and military strength of the United States had immediately and decisively swung the balance of power toward the Allies. With each passing month, the military position of Germany and the other Central Powers became less stable. One by one, Germany's allies gave up the fight, and on November 11, 1918, Germany signed an agreement with the Allies that was essentially an unconditional surrender.

War and Progress

Progressive leaders in America had been divided over the issue of entering World War I. Supporters of the idea, such as Social Gospel leader Lyman Abbott and journalist Walter Lippmann, argued that by joining the fight against a dictator's regime in Germany, Americans would be encouraged and inspired to support Progressive reforms at home. "We shall turn with fresh interest to our own tyrannies— to our Colorado mines, our [powerful] steel industries, our sweatshops and our slums,"[45] Lippmann predicted.

Other Progressive leaders condemned America's entrance into the war. Some critics, such as the influential Jane Addams, opposed this decision because of their personal reservations against violence. They formed an important part of a vocal peace movement within America during this time. Others feared that the war would give too much power back to American industry, which would be responsible for supplying the U.S. military with airplanes, ships, ammunition, uniforms, and countless other supplies. Many of these same skeptics also worried that the war effort would distract America from its serious domestic problems.

Initially, it appeared that these fears would not come to pass. In fact, some historians regard the months of American involvement in World War I as the absolute height of the Progressive Era. As American soldiers fought overseas to make the

Silencing Critics

In 1918, the U.S. Congress passed and enacted the Sedition Act. This controversial legislation imposed jail sentences and heavy fines on any American who dared to write, publish, or say anything that criticized the U.S. government while the nation was at war. This law, which was a blatant violation of the First Amendment of the U.S. Bill of Rights that guaranteed free speech, was used to silence a large number of pacifists and other critics of America's involvement in World War I.

The most famous use of the Sedition Act came against Eugene V. Debs, the labor organizer and activist. He had run for president in 1900, 1904, 1908, and 1912. An outspoken pacifist and opponent of U.S. involvement in World War I, Debs gave an anti-war speech in June 1918 in Canton, Ohio. Under the Sedition Act, he was arrested, tried, and sentenced to 10 years in prison. Debs appealed the decision, and the case eventually reached the U.S. Supreme Court. In a shocking turn of events, the Supreme Court upheld his conviction. Not intimidated, Debs launched yet another presidential campaign from his prison cell in 1920. One year later, Congress repealed the Sedition Act, and Debs's sentence was considered null and void.

Controversial and influential, Eugene V. Debs was never afraid to speak out about his beliefs. This got him in serious trouble under the Sedition Act of 1918 when he criticized the Great War.

world safe and spread democracy, the administration of Woodrow Wilson worked tirelessly to create a wartime model for a peacetime Progressive utopia. Against the backdrop of struggle and sacrifice, reformers succeeded in outlawing alcohol, winning suffrage for women, expanding the income tax, and taking over the railroads.

By the time America emerged on the victorious side of the Great War, however, the American public had decided that the federal government now had access to too much control over the American economy and society. The voices calling for resistance to Progressivism quickly became so loud and sustained that even President Wilson was forced to acknowledge them and change his approach to governing. "Rather than an advertisement for a progressive future," one scholar wrote, "the Wilsonian war effort became the death knell [sign of demise] for the progressive movement."[46]

Turning Away

In addition to the Progressive movement's leaders' disagreements over World War I, several other factors drove Americans away from the ideas that had dominated the nation's politics for nearly two decades. Economic anxiety was one big issue. The cost of paying for the war led the Wilson administration to raise taxes on the middle class, which in turn, set off a wave of inflation that frightened poor, working-class, and middle-class Americans. Though the war increased employment in nearly all industries, the prices of common goods also increased. This was scary for the poorest classes, who were afraid that they would not be able to afford food once the war ended.

Another issue was the war's role in changing public opinions about American business. For decades, large portions of the American population had seen the nation's corporations as ruthless giants that crushed everything—and everyone—in their path. Similarly, they regarded the country's leading industrialists as coldhearted businessmen with an unquenchable thirst for money. However, after the United States entered World War I, government agencies, newspapers, magazines, and corporate spokesmen alike praised the role of American industry in outfitting the nation's armed forces. After the outbreak of war, many people realized that even though America's factories, railroads, and banks had a troubled past and sometimes still engaged in unfair practices, they were still a tremendous national asset.

The Wilson administration also made several decisions to restrict basic constitutional freedoms during the war. This led many Americans to conclude that government regulations and oversight of society were reaching unhealthy levels. The administration decided to impose a mandatory draft to fill up the military ranks. This meant that all qualified citizens—mostly young, unmarried men—were required to serve in the armed forces. This was enormously unpopular in most parts of the country. The Justice Department also secretly organized a group of

250,000 civilians into a pro-war group called the American Protective League. This group was active in 600 American cities, and its members reported on suspected spies, German sympathizers, and people who failed to buy war bonds or show enthusiasm for the war.

In addition, the government passed a number of substantial war measures designed to silence or imprison anyone who obstructed the war effort. These laws included the Sedition Act, which made it illegal to say anything negative about the American government's war effort; the Espionage Act, which prohibited any American from sharing information that could obstruct the armed forces; and the Trading with the Enemy Act, which restricted the ability of people to trade with other countries. Critics believed that by passing such laws, the Wilson administration was trampling on the same democratic ideals that it was supposedly fighting to defend.

Many Americans were caught up in the patriotic spirit of wartime, and they dismissed these accusations. Instead, they spent more of their energy supporting the war effort. Some also made outspoken opponents of the war, such as anarchist Emma Goldman, Socialist Party leader Eugene V. Debs, and IWW president "Big" Bill Haywood, look bad. Even mainstream opponents of the war, who were similar to Addams, were condemned as anti-American. In the opinion of many supporters of America's entrance into the conflict of World War I, anyone who questioned the war was guilty of treason.

As the fighting went on, though, even steadfast supporters of the war were getting angry with the rising number of government-imposed restrictions on business practices and private behavior. According to this perspective, "every male between 18 and 45 had been deprived of freedom of his body," stated journalist and historian Mark Sullivan.

Every person had been deprived of freedom of his tongue ... Every business man [no longer controlled] his factory or store, every housewife surrendered control of her table, every farmer was forbidden to sell his wheat except at the price the government fixed ... in six months, in America the state took back, the individual gave up, what had taken centuries of [fighting] to win.[47]

Another important factor in the decline of Progressivism was the death of Theodore Roosevelt in 1919, just a few months after World War I ended. Roosevelt's passing deprived the Progressive movement of its most popular, outspoken, and successful champion. In addition to the end of the war in 1918, Roosevelt's death seemed like a powerful omen that the Age of Reform was coming to an abrupt end.

Changing Times

World War I had left many of the oldest European powers in terrible condition, but the United States emerged from the war with a roaring economy and citizens

Extreme Labor

Throughout American labor history, few individuals were both loved and hated as much as "Big" Bill Haywood, the radical activist who led the IWW for much of the Progressive Era. Born in Salt Lake City, Utah, in 1869, Haywood was raised in poverty. His father died when he was three years old, and he was working in the mines by the time he was nine years old.

Haywood's life as a labor organizer began in the mid-1890s when he became a leader of an Idaho chapter of the Western Federation of Miners. Within a few years, he had emerged as a leading figure in the national union—serving on the union's General Executive Board by 1900—and one of the most radical voices for labor rights in the American West. In 1905, Haywood helped found the IWW. This group argued for increased workers' rights and fair treatment, which were both popular topics at the time. However, they were also largely socialist, meaning they did not agree with the American system of economy. This made most citizens distrust them.

One year later, Haywood was charged with plotting the assassination of former Idaho governor Frank Steunenberg. He was cleared of the charges, and he returned to a leadership position in the IWW, where he created controversy with his fiery condemnations of big business. In 1915, he became the official head of the IWW. After the Russian Revolution of 1917, Haywood and other Wobblies expressed open support for Vladimir Lenin and his Communist regime. This support, combined with Haywood's outspoken disagreement with America's involvement in World War I, made him a target of the federal government. In 1917, Haywood and 100 other IWW supporters were arrested by

that were excited—and enriched—by the thrill of victory. With a powerful economy came excess spending money, and Americans rushed to stores to buy the new consumer products being created by the nation's booming corporations. These large companies had emerged from the war with enormous sums of money, which they invested in new factories, new machinery, and campaign contributions for politicians who they hoped to influence. Once the nation's soldiers returned home, Americans delighted in the belief that their nation was the world's newest financial and military superpower.

However, the end of the Great War also brought new uncertainties and

authorities and charged with violating the Espionage and Sedition Acts. He was convicted, but he remained free on bail while his appeals were heard. When the Supreme Court rejected his appeal in 1921, Haywood fled to the Soviet Union, where he died in 1928.

As one of the founders of the radical IWW, "Big" Bill Haywood was a prominent figure in 1900s America.

challenges. During the war, African Americans from the South had moved into northern cities to work in the factories and shipyards that operated at maximum capacity to provide American troops with ships, guns, uniforms, blankets, and other supplies. Once the war ended, though, white soldiers returned home and needed to find new jobs. Factories had fewer jobs and more people asking for them. Competition for employment during this period was intense. African Americans almost always lost these struggles because of widespread racism and discrimination across America. Even as many African Americans lost their jobs, incidents of white violence against blacks soared in many parts of the country. Racial tensions were reaching new highs.

The wartime demand for factory workers and other laborers also bolstered the ranks of many unions. Powerful labor organizations, such as the AFL, saw their membership rise by nearly 1 million. The AFL and other growing unions prevented themselves from confronting corporations over work issues while America was at war. After the conflict ended, though, the labor movement moved quickly to capture its share of the economic riches that were spreading throughout postwar America. When corporate leaders rejected many of these demands, labor unrest exploded across the country. In 1919, hundreds of thousands of worker across dozens of different industries participated in strikes.

Many of these strikes failed, however, in large part because management succeeded in branding strikers as Bolshevik agents or sympathizers. The Bolsheviks were Russian Communists who, in 1917's Russian Revolution, had overthrown Czar Nicholas II and created a Communist government headed by

The Russian Revolution marked the first time a major power converted to Communist rule. Vladimir Lenin, shown here, was the world's first major Communist leader.

Vladimir Lenin.

The bloody Russian Revolution, which culminated in the execution of Nicholas II and his entire royal family, greatly alarmed the United States. The new Communist regime fiercely opposed private property, capitalism, and individual rights. Instead, Lenin and his Bolshevik supporters were dedicated to establishing a classless political system in which the state controlled all aspects of the economy and society. The Bolsheviks also pledged that Communism would soon sweep over the rest of the world.

Against Communism

American fear and distrust of Russia surged after the war, when many Americans began to associate Communism with two controversial portions of the U.S. population: labor union members and immigrants. The American labor movement and many of the nation's recent immigrants did have similar, but less extreme, political beliefs as the Bolsheviks. Their calls for social justice and condemnations of greedy corporate capitalism even echoed some of the language used by Lenin and other Communist leaders. In addition, some high-profile labor groups, such as the IWW, proudly campaigned for Communist solutions to America's problems. Finally, many Americans were still angry about the anti-war positions that some labor leaders and immigrants had taken during World War I.

Because of the eye-popping red color of the Communist flag, many Russians and their sympathizers were called "Reds." As fears that Reds were infiltrating America spread all across the country, many immigrants and labor leaders tried to reassure the public of their patriotism. They pointed out that fighting social injustice and corporate abuses was not the same as advocating for the overthrow of the American political system. They also noted that union members and immigrants, who fought as soldiers and manned the wartime assembly lines, had played an important role in defeating Germany in the Great War.

These efforts had little impact, however. Instead, the United States gave in to fear and paranoia, and the notorious Red Scare of 1919 and 1920 swept across the land. During these months, immigrants and unions were targeted for raids, intimidation, and violence. In an effort to cripple unions and maximize corporate profits, many large companies effectively promoted the idea that labor organizations were strongholds of Communist sympathizers. When midwestern steel workers launched a general strike in 1919, for example, company owners successfully portrayed the strikers—many of whom were immigrants—as dangerous radicals who threatened the American way of life.

This corporate strategy worked for a number of different companies facing strikes. Striking workers were upset at the attacks on their patriotism, but their protests were drowned out by corporate propaganda and newspaper editorials that said that calls for better wages and working conditions

Writing About Progress

As a Progressive editor and author, Herbert David Croly founded a journal called *The New Republic* and wrote several highly respected books on American politics and culture. Because of his influential writings, he is frequently cited as one of the creators of modern liberalism in America. Born on January 23, 1869, in New York City, Croly attended Harvard University and spent most of his life as a writer and editor.

Croly did not achieve a national reputation, though, until the Progressive Era was in full swing. In 1909, he published *The Promise of American Life*, in which he explained his belief that both a strong national government and strong individual rights could coexist in a democratic society. The book reportedly made a significant impression on Theodore Roosevelt, the foremost Progressive politician of the age, as well as other political leaders, including Woodrow Wilson. In 1914, he founded *The New Republic*, which quickly became the nation's best-known Progressive magazine. Croly remained the editor of *The New Republic* until his death on May 17, 1930. Today, Croly's works survive as enduring influences in modern American liberal political thought.

better wages and working conditions were the same as Communism. "[You cannot be] a loyal American unless … you give up all the rights your country gives you and obey your employer,"[48] one worker despaired. Millions of other union supporters felt like they were trapped in another impossible situation: They either had to accept the abuses of corporations or be labeled Communist sympathizers.

The End of an Era

Labor union members and other victims of the Red Scare turned to President Wilson's administration for help, but they were turned away. By this time, Wilson and many other American politicians had changed their policies to fit in with the shifting political ideas of the time. They did not want to be viewed as sympathetic to groups that were distrusted by so many American voters.

Moreover, much of Wilson's attention was elsewhere. In 1919, he devoted nearly all of his energy to generating support in Washington for the newly founded League of Nations, an international body designed to use diplomacy to prevent future wars. In

October 1919, however, he suffered a stroke that limited his ability to campaign for the League. In the end, the U.S. Congress never ratified the agreement, and the United States never joined the League, despite the fact that it was mostly Wilson's idea.

Even before his stroke, however, Wilson had distanced himself from the Progressive movement, which many Americans now linked with Communist labor radicals and immigrant troublemakers. By 1920, most Americans seemed to want the Progressives, who had been celebrated during the last few decades for exposing the nation's social problems, to just go away. "To question the wisdom of the powers that be, to advance new and disturbing ideas, had ceased to be an act of virtue, the proof of an aspiring spirit," famed Progressive lawyer Donald Richberg wrote. "Such attitudes were [now] 'radical' and 'destructive.' Progressivism was losing its supreme asset—respectability"[49]

The presidential election of November 1920 was the first time women in America were allowed to vote in a national election. The federal support for woman suffrage was one of the Progressive Era's greatest achievements. However, this same election cemented the downfall of the Age of Reform. The Republican ticket of

Near the end of his presidency, Woodrow Wilson spent most of his time rallying support for his League of Nations, as he is here, instead of advocating for Progressive reform.

Warren G. Harding and Calvin Coolidge decisively defeated Democratic nominee James Cox and his running mate, future president Franklin D. Roosevelt. Harding and Coolidge were outspoken defenders of American business, and they vowed to loosen governmental supervision of the American economy and restore stability to daily American life.

Progressing Toward the Future

During the 1920s, Progressive forces in America were in full retreat. Courts and lawmakers alike worked to reduce regulations that managed corporate behavior and repeal laws meant to address poverty and other social problems. The Roaring Twenties also saw American culture emphasize pleasure, excess spending money, and personal freedom like never before. In this period of general middle-class prosperity, many Americans were not interested in hearing about the continued struggles of the poor or the ways in which corporate powers had regained their influence over the country's politicians.

Then, the collapse of the stock market in 1929 marked the beginning of the Great Depression, which shook America and the world. This terrible economic downturn caused massive job losses across the United States and financially ruined millions of families. Confronted by this extreme threat to the nation, President Franklin D. Roosevelt, who was elected for the first time in 1932, immediately responded by instituting the New Deal. This ambitious set of federal programs reflected Roosevelt's belief that the Great Depression could not be beaten without the active intervention of the national government.

During the New Deal era, which lasted until the early 1940s, the Roosevelt administration passed new banking reform laws, funded work and agricultural relief programs, gave new protections to unions and other working Americans, established the Social Security pension system for elderly and disabled Americans, and introduced numerous other initiatives to help struggling Americans. In short, Roosevelt and the New Deal drew upon the example and spirit of the Progressive Era to defend the American people from the massive unemployment and economic turmoil of the Great Depression.

Since that time, the shadow of the Progressive Era has shifted in influence over the United States. "From 1960 to 1980, America experienced sharp swings between the progressive and conservative approaches," wrote one scholar. "But it also experienced periods of political stalemate when progressives and conservatives fought to a draw."[50] Despite these political swings, the federal government has remained an important part of daily American life for nearly a century. In this regard, the influence of the Progressive movement has never truly faded.

This influence has been hotly

debated over the years. Conservatives believe that excessive government authority has unfairly limited personal liberties, eroded traditions of self-reliance and independence, and hampered economic growth that could benefit all Americans. President Ronald Reagan famously summarized this viewpoint in 1981 when he declared that government was not a solution to the problems of the American people, but rather that a large government was itself the cause of the nation's problems.

Liberal political thinkers profoundly disagree with this assessment. To the contrary, they feel that government involvement in the affairs of American society and business has helped—and continues to help—the nation grow and prosper. As Progressive historian Arthur J. Schlesinger wrote at the start of the 21st century,

The record surely shows that the intervention of national authority ... has given a majority of Americans more personal dignity and liberty than they ever had before. The individual freedoms destroyed have been ... the freedom to deny black Americans their elementary rights as American citizens, the freedom to work little children in mills and immigrants in sweatshops, the freedom to pay starvation wages and enforce dawn-to-dusk working hours and permit [terrible] working conditions, the freedom to deceive in the sale of goods and securities and drugs, the freedom to loot national resources and pollute the environment, and so on. These are all freedoms ... that a civilized country can readily do without.[51]

Notes

Introduction:
From Industry to Progress

1. Michael McGerr, *A Fierce Discontent: The Rise and Fall of the Progressive Movement in America*. New York, NY: Oxford University Press, 2005, pp. 4, 6.

Chapter One:
Increasing Industrialism

2. Alex Groner and Editors of *Business Week and American Heritage, The American Heritage History of American Business and Industry*. New York, NY: American Heritage, 1972, p. 11.
3. McGerr, *A Fierce Discontent*, p. 8.
4. Quoted in McGerr, *A Fierce Discontent*, p. 8.
5. Benjamin Harrison, *Views of an Ex-President: Being His Addresses and Writings on Subjects of Public Interest Since the Close of His Administration as President of the United States*. Indianapolis, IN: Bowen-Merrill Company, 1901, p. 336.
6. David Traxel, *Crusader Nation: The United States in Peace and the Great War 1898–1920*. New York, NY: Alfred A. Knopf, 2006, p. 6.
7. John Mitchell, "An Exposition and Interpretation of the Trade Union Movement," in *The Christian Ministry and the Social Order*, ed. Charles S. McFarland. New Haven, CT: Yale University Press, 1913, p. 90.
8. Traxel, *Crusader Nation*, p. 9.
9. William Allen White, *The Autobiography of William Allen White*. New York, NY: Macmillan, 1946, p. 390.
10. Quoted in Clarence Darrow, *Verdicts out of Court*, eds. Arthur Weinberg and Lila Weinberg. Chicago, IL: Elephant Paperbacks, 1989, p. 64.

Chapter Two:
Society and Politics

11. James N. Gregory, *The Southern Diaspora: How the Great Migrations of Black and White Southerners Transformed America*. Chapel Hill, NC: University of North Carolina Press, 2007, p. 23.
12. Anthony Lukas, *Big Trouble: A Murder in a Small Western Town Sets Off a Struggle for the Soul of America*. New York, NY: Simon & Schuster, 1997, p. 305.
13. Quoted in William Cronon, *Nature's Metropolis: Chicago and the Great West*. New York, NY: Norton, 1991, p. 9.
14. Traxel, *Crusader Nation*, p. 9.
15. Quoted in Robert S. Gallagher, "I Was Arrested, Of Course ..." *American Heritage*. February

1974. www.americanheritage.com/content/%E2%80%9Ci-was-arresed-course%E2%80%A6%E2%80%9D?page=show.

16. Quoted in McGerr, *A Fierce Discontent*, p. 84.

17. Roger A. Bruns, *Preacher: Billy Sunday and Big-Time American Evangelism*. New York, NY: W.W. Norton, 1992, p. 161.

18. Quoted in Aaron Barlow, *The Depression Era*. Santa Barbara, CA: Greenwood, 2016, p. 41.

19. Quoted in Paul S. Boyer, *Urban Masses and Moral Order in America: 1820–1920*. Cambridge, MA: Harvard University Press, 1978, p. 208.

20. Quoted in McGerr, *A Fierce Discontent*, p. 88.

21. Quoted in McGerr, *A Fierce Discontent*, p. 192.

22. McGerr, *A Fierce Discontent*, p. 235.

Chapter Three: Big Business and Little Labor

23. McGerr, *A Fierce Discontent*, p. 16.

24. Stephen Yafa, *Cotton: The Biography of a Revolutionary Fiber*. New York, NY: Penguin, 2005, p. 94.

25. Quoted in Smithsonian Source, "Quote from a Pullman laborer, 1883," Smithsonian Source. www.smithsoniansource.org/display/primarysource/viewdetails.aspx?PrimarySourceId=1221.

26. Robert H. Zieger, Timothy J. Minchin, and Gilbert J. Gall, *American Workers, American Unions: The Twentieth and Early Twenty-first Centuries*. Baltimore, MD: Johns Hopkins University Press, 1986, p. 3.

27. John Steele Gordon, *An Empire of Wealth: The Epic History of American Economic Power*. New York, NY: HarperCollins, 2004, p. 250.

28. Quoted in Ralph Darlington, *Syndicalism and the Transition to Communism: An International Comparative Analysis*. Hampshire, UK: Ashgate, 2008, p. 22.

29. Jane Addams, "The Settlement as a Factor in the Labor Movement," in *Hull House Maps and Papers: A Presentation of Nationalities and Wages in a Congested District of Chicago, Together with Comments and Essays on Problems Growing out of the Social Conditions* by Residents of Hull-House. New York, NY: Thomas Y. Crowell & Co., 1895, p. 204.

30. McGerr, *A Fierce Discontent*, p. 143.

31. Rufus Wheeler Peckham, *Lochner v. People of State of New York, 198 U.S. 45 (1905)*. The opinion of the Supreme Court of the United States, decided April 17, 1905. law2.umkc.edu/faculty/PROJECTS/FTRIALS/conlaw/lochner.html.

32. Quoted in Elliott J. Gorn, *Mother Jones: The Most Dangerous Woman in America*. New York, NY: Hill and Wang, 2001, p. 216.

Chapter Four: Presidential Policies

33. Quoted in Paul M. Rego, *American Ideal: Theodore Roosevelt's Search for*

American Individualism. Plymouth, UK: Lexington Books, 2008, p. 65.

34. Quoted in Edmund Morris, *The Rise of Theodore Roosevelt*. New York, NY: Modern Library, 2001, p. 513.

35. Theodore Roosevelt, "Theodore Roosevelt: First Annual Message, December 3rd, 1901." The American Presidency Project. www.presidency.ucsb.edu/ws/?pid=29542.

36. Robert L. Reynolds, "The Coal Kings Come to Judgment," *American Heritage*, April 1960. www.americanheritage.com/content/coal-kings-come-judgment.

37. Quoted in Traxel, *Crusader Nation*, p. 21.

38. Morris, *The Rise of Theodore Roosevelt*, p. xxvii.

39. Traxel, *Crusader Nation*, p. 12.

40. Theodore Roosevelt, *An Autobiography*. New York, NY: Macmillan, 1919, p. 302.

41. Theodore Roosevelt, "National Unity Versus Class Cleavage," in *The Writings of Theodore Roosevelt*, ed. William H. Harbaugh. Indianapolis, IN: Bobbs-Merrill, 1967, p. 20.

42. Theodore Roosevelt, "The Man with the Muck-Rake," in *50 Greatest Speeches of the World*. New Delhi, India: Ocean Books, 2014, p. 338.

43. Aida D. Donald, *Lion in the White House: A Life of Theodore Roosevelt*. New York, NY: Basic Books, 2007, p. 193.

44. Woodrow Wilson, *The New Freedom: A Call for Emancipation of the Generous Energies of a People* (1913). Charleston, SC: BiblioBazaar, 2007, p. 14.

Epilogue: No End to Progress

45. Quoted in Alan Dawley, *Struggles for Justice; Social Responsibility and the Liberal State*. Cambridge, MA: Belknap Press, 1991, p. 196.

46. McGerr, *A Fierce Discontent*, p. 281.

47. Quoted in McGerr, *A Fierce Discontent*, p. 302.

48. Quoted in John C. Hennen, *The Americanization of West Virginia: Creating a Modern Industrial State 1916–1925*. Lexington, KY: University Press of Kentucky, 1996, p. 81.

49. Quoted in Kevin C. Murphy, "Chapter Six: Legacies of the Scare: Progressives, Civil Liberties, and Labor," KevinCMurphy.com. www.kevincmurphy.com/uatw-legacies-addams.html.

50. John B. Judis, "Are We All Progressives Now?," *American Prospect*, December 19, 2001. prospect.org/article/are-we-all-progressives-now.

51. Arthur M. Schlesinger Jr., "A Question of Power," *American Prospect*, December 19, 2001. prospect.org/article/question-power.

For More Information

Books

Berkin, Carol. *Making America, Vol. 2: Since 1865: A History of the United States*. Boston, MA: Wadsworth, 2012. Stretching back to before the Industrial Revolution, this detailed and thoroughly researched text presents a broad look at how the currents of history came together to both create the Progressive Era and cause its downfall.

Clift, Eleanor. *Founding Sisters and the 19th Amendment*. Hoboken, NJ: Wiley, 2003. This book chronicles the struggle for woman suffrage in America, one of the Progressive Era's proudest feats, from the mid-1800s all the way to the passage of the 19th Amendment.

Jaycox, Faith. *The Progressive Era: An Eyewitness History*. New York, NY: Facts On File, 2005. This book looks at the Progressive Era from a wide range of perspectives, including workers, managers, suffragists, and prohibitionists.

McGerr, Michael. *A Fierce Discontent: The Rise and Fall of the Progressive Movement in America*. New York, NY: Oxford University Press, 2005. A fast-paced and informative overview of the Progressive Era and its leading champions, this book includes both primary sources and expert commentary by an experienced historian.

Remes, Jacob A.C. *Disaster Citizenship: Survivors, Solidarity, and Power in the Progressive Era*. Urbana, IL: University of Illinois Press, 2016. This book details some of the tragic events that inspired the Progressive movement in the 1910s and how Americans dealt with an unsafe work environment.

Sicius, Francis J. *The Progressive Era: A Reference Guide*. Santa Barbara, CA: ABC-CLIO, 2015. This detailed overview includes discussions of the important dates and events of the Progressive Era in American history, as well as profiles of its important figures.

Websites

**America 1900
(www.pbs.org/wgbh/amex/1900)**
This multimedia site is a companion
to a film in the PBS *American Experience* series; it has links to the film
itself, informative articles, and a
useful timeline.

**"The New Progressive Movement"
(www.nytimes.com/2011/11/13/
opinion/sunday/the-new-
progressive-movement.html)**
This lengthy and well-researched
article links the motivations of the
American Progressive Era in the 1900s
to the current political trends across
the country, examining how the past
connects to the present.

**The 1911 Triangle Factory Fire
(www.ilr.cornell.edu/trianglefire)**
This site, maintained by Cornell University, provides a wealth
of information about the infamous 1911 fire, which came to be
a national symbol of corporate
exploitation of American workers
and a rallying cry for Progressivism.

**Overview of the Progressive Era
(www.digitalhistory.uh.edu/era.
cfm?eraid=11)**
Part of a digital historical encyclopedia, this site has a quick look at the
time period around the Progressive
movement, as well as links to
the other important events that
influenced it.

**Urban Experience in Chicago: Hull-
House and Its Neighborhoods,
1889–1963
(www.uic.edu/jaddams/hull/
urbanexp)**
Created by the University of Illinois at
Chicago, this site provides multimedia
coverage, including images and
primary source documents, of Jane
Addams, her successful settlement
house, and the wider issue of urban
poverty in America.

Index

A

Abbott, Lyman, 80
abortion, 40
Adamson Act (1916), 77
Addams, Jane
   child labor and, 40
   settlement house movement and, 9,
     38–39
   Theodore Roosevelt and, 41
   unions and, 57
   World War I and, 80, 83
African Americans
   Jim Crow laws in South, 31–32, 46
   migration to Northern cities, 85
   segregation as solution to race prob-
     lems, 30, 46
   unions and, 54, 56
agriculture, 20, 30
alcohol, 6, 37, 43–45, 66, 82
Altgeld, John Peter, 26
American Federation of Labor (AFL)
   early unions in, 52
   unskilled workers and, 53
   women and, 54, 57, 59
   World War I, 86
American Protective League, 83
American Railway Union, 27
American Sugar Refining Company, 25
American West, settlement of, 13–14
anarchists, 83
Anti-Saloon League, 6, 43–44

B

Baker, Purley A., 44
Biltmore Estate, 19–20
birth control, 40
Bitter Cry of the Children, The (Spargo), 51

Bolsheviks, 86–87
"Booze Sermon" (Sunday), 43
"bread and roses," 57
Bryan, William Jennings, 22, 66
Bull Moose Party, 40

C

capitalism, 16, 56, 87
Carnegie, Andrew, 16–17, 19
Chicago
   Haymarket Riot, 25–26
   Hull House, 9, 38–39
   living conditions in, 32
   political corruption, 36–37
   Pullman Strike, 26–27
child labor
   government regulation, 8, 37, 40, 54
   Keating-Owen Act on, 40
   mines and, 51, 69
Cigar Makers' International Union
   (CMIU), 55
civil service, 21
Civil Service Act, 24
Civil Service Commission, 66
class conflict
   survival of the fittest and, 15
   as threat to existence of United
     States, 8–9, 27
Clayton Antitrust Act (1914), 76–77
Cleveland, Grover, 27
coal mining
   child labor, 51, 69
   strikes, 69
   union, 6, 54
   working conditions in, 50–51
Colorado Fuel and Iron Company, 62
Communists, 71, 84, 86–89

company towns, 50
conservation, 7, 74–75
Constitution
    17th Amendment (1913), 36
    18th Amendment (1920), 11, 44–45
    19th Amendment (1920), 11, 42–43
    21st Amendment (1933), 45
Coolidge, Calvin, 90
corporations
    mergers to create giant, 59
    regulation after Theodore Roosevelt, 76–77
    regulation before Theodore Roosevelt, 25
    regulation by federal government from 1891 to 1920 of, 53, 59, 61
    Theodore Roosevelt and, 60, 68, 70–71, 73–74
    welfare capitalism, 72
    World War I and, 82
    See also mining industry; railroads
courts
    injunctions and, 53, 77
    laissez-faire philosophy, 61
    See also Supreme Court
Cox, James, 90
Croly, Herbert David, 88

D
Darrow, Clarence, 27, 29
Darwin, Charles, 15
Debs, Eugene V.
    as presidential candidate, 71, 81
    as president of American Railway Union, 27
    World War I and, 81, 83
Department of Agriculture, 20
depression of 1890s, 25, 54
draft, 82
DuBois, W.E.B., 46

E
economy
    capitalism, 16, 56, 87
    depression of 1890s, 25, 54
    Great Depression, 45, 90
    Industrial Revolution and, 10, 12, 48, 59, 73
    laissez-faire philosophy, 61
    robber barons and, 18
    welfare capitalism, 72
elections
    1892, 22
    1896, 22
    1900, 66–67, 81
    1904, 70–71, 81
    1908, 64, 81
    1912, 64, 75, 78, 81
    1920, 81, 89–90
electoral reforms, 35–36
England, 8, 12–13, 49, 55, 79

F
factory workers
    children, 33, 38, 48–49
    safety laws in New York, 61, 63
    Triangle Shirtwaist Factory fire, 7, 61–63
    working conditions, 49–50
farming. *See* agriculture
Federal Children's Bureau, 40
Federal Trade Commission Act (1914), 76
Franz Ferdinand (archduke of Austria), 79

G
Gilded Age, 18–19, 24, 59
Gompers, Samuel, 52, 55, 57
government, federal
    corruption, 24, 35, 60
    debate over role of, 10, 71, 73, 76, 82
    direct election of senators, 21, 36

food safety regulations, 37
ownership of railroads and communication, 21
Populist party and, 21–22
railroads and, 27
service system created, 24
trusts and, 7, 25, 29, 59–60, 67, 69, 71, 76
Granger movement, 20–21
Great Depression, 45, 90
Great War, 78, 80–82, 84, 87
greed, 16, 18–19, 24, 37, 50, 60, 65, 72, 87

H
Harding, Warren G., 90
Harrison, Benjamin, 16
Haymarket Riot (1886), 25–26, 54
Haywood, "Big" Bill, 56, 83–85
Henry Street Settlement House, 40
Hepburn Act (1906), 7, 73
How the Other Half Lives (Riis), 6, 36
Hull House, 9, 38–39

I
immigrants
    as labor source, 13–14
    Populist desire to restrict, 21
    Red Scare and, 87
    settlement houses and, 37–39
    settlement of American West, 13–14
    sources of, 13–14, 32
income gap, 23
income tax, 21, 82
individualism, 16
Industrial Revolution
    American embrace of, 12
    effect on people, 10
    need for government action as result, 48, 59, 73
Industrial Workers of the World, "Wobblies" (IWW), 54, 56–57, 83–85

injunctions, 53, 77
International Typographical Union, 52
Interstate Commerce Commission (ICC), 25, 73
inventions, 12

J
Jim Crow laws, 31–32, 46
Johnson, Hiram, 35
Jones, Mary Harris "Mother," 10, 56, 62
journalists, 10, 36–37, 46, 51, 63, 68, 71, 75, 80, 83
Jungle, The (Sinclair), 7, 37

K
Keating Owen Child Labor Act (1916), 40
Kelley, Oliver Hudson, 20
Knights of Labor, 54

L
La Follette, Robert M., 35, 58, 63
laissez-faire philosophy, 61
League of Nations, 75, 89
liberalism, 88
Lippmann, Walter, 80
living conditions
    of wealthy, 18–20
    of working class, 32–33, 50–51
Lochner era, 61
Lochner v. New York (1905), 61
Ludlow Massacre (1914), 61–63

M
Mann-Elkins Act (1910), 76
manufacturing workers. *See* factory workers
McKinley, William, 22, 64, 66–67
Meat Inspection Act (1906), 37
middle class
    desire for reforms, 23–24, 36, 63
    during Roaring Twenties, 90

muckrakers and, 36
  social Darwinism and, 15–16
  Social Gospel movement and, 24
  Theodore Roosevelt and, 70
  unions and, 52
  Woodrow Wilson and, 82
mining industry
  child labor, 6, 51
  injunctions and, 53
  Ludlow Massacre, 61–63
  1902 strike, 69–70
  Theodore Roosevelt's conservation
    efforts and, 74–75
  union, 54
  working conditions, 50–51
Mitchell, John, 20, 53–54, 70
moral responsibility, sense of, 24
Morgan, J.P., 17–19, 59, 68–69
muckrakers, 7, 36, 51, 63, 68

N
National American Woman Suffrage
  Association (NAWSA), 41
National Labor Union, 54
New Deal, 90
"New Nationalism" (Theodore Roos-
  evelt), 60
New Republic, The (magazine), 88
New York City, 61, 65–66, 88
Nobel Peace Prize, 38
Norris, Frank, 36–37
Norris-LaGuardia Act (1931), 53
Northern Securities Company, 6, 69

O
Octopus, The (Norris), 37
oil industry, 28–29, 76
Owen, Robert, 40, 42

P
Parker, Alton B., 71
Paul, Alice, 10, 41

Pendleton, George H., 24
Pendleton Civil Service Act (1883), 24
philanthropy, 17, 29
political corruption
  political machines and, 35–36
  Populists target, 21
  reform measures, 22–23
  The Shame of the Cities and, 36
political machines, 35–36
Prohibition, 6, 11, 35, 43–45
Promise of American Life, The (Croly), 88
Pullman Palace Car Company, 27, 51
Pure Food and Drug Act (1906), 37

R
railroads
  Adamson Act and, 77
  Carnegie, Andrew and, 17
  deaths on the job, 49
  government regulation, 25, 73
  J.P. Morgan and, 68–69
  Populist demand for government
    ownership, 21
  unions and, 27
Reagan, Ronald, 91
Red Scare (1919 to 1920), 7, 87–88
referendum, 35–36
Richberg, Donald, 89
Riis, Jacob, 6, 36
Roaring Twenties, 45, 90
robber barons, 18
Rockefeller, John D., 19, 28–29, 68–69
Roosevelt, Franklin D., 90
Roosevelt, Theodore
  background before presidency, 65–66
  beliefs, 73
  conservation, 7, 74–75
  death, 83
  election of 1912 and, 40–41, 60, 75
  food safety and, 37
  governing style of, 66–67
  influences on, 88

muckrakers and, 36, 68
"new nationalism" and, 60
popularity of, 70
prohibition of alcohol and, 44
sworn in as president, 67
trusts and, 29, 69, 71
woman suffrage and, 40–41
"Rough Riders," 66
Russian Revolution, 7, 84, 86–87

S
Sanger, Margaret, 40
Schlesinger, Arthur J., 91
Sedition Act (1918), 81, 83, 85
segregation, 30, 32, 46–47
settlement house movement, 37–40
Shame of the Cities, The (Steffens), 36
Sherman Antitrust Act (1890), 6, 25, 69, 77
Sinclair, Upton, 7, 10, 37, 68
slums, 20, 23, 32, 36–37, 70, 73, 80
social Darwinism, 15–16
Social Gospel movement, 24, 37, 46, 80
Spanish-American War (1898), 66
Spargo, John, 51
Spencer, Herbert, 15
Square Deal, 7, 60, 71
Standard Oil Trust, 29, 76
Starr, Ellen Gates, 38
steel industry, 8, 13, 17, 31, 50, 52, 59, 72, 80, 87
Steffens, Lincoln, 36
Steunenberg, Frank, 84
Stevenson, Adlai E., 66
strikes
    against mine owners, 6, 61–63, 69–70
    American Railway Union against Pullman Palace Car Company, 26–27
    Clayton Act and, 77
    Haymarket Riot and, 25–26, 54
    Knights of Labor and, 54

Ludlow Massacre and, 62–63
Red Scare and, 7, 87–88
Strong, Josiah, 46
suffrage, 10, 35, 38, 40–42, 58, 82, 90
Sullivan, Mark, 83
Sumner, William Graham, 15
Sunday, Billy, 10, 43
Supreme Court
    Haywood, "Big" Bill and, 85
    regulation of corporations decisions, 21, 25, 29, 61, 69, 76
    Standard Oil Trust decision, 29, 76
    working conditions decision, 61
"survival of the fittest" concept, 15

T
Taft, William, 44, 46, 64, 75–76, 78
taxes, income, 21, 82
temperance movement, 37, 43
tenements, 6, 20, 32–33, 36, 39, 43
trade unions, 37, 40, 53, 55, 57
transportation, 36
Triangle Shirtwaist Factory fire (1911), 7, 61–63
Trotter, Monroe, 46
trusts
    failure to control, 25
    oil, 29, 76
    Theodore Roosevelt and, 7, 29, 60, 67, 69, 71

U
unions
    attempts to represent all workers, 54
    injunctions and, 53
    mining and, 6, 53–54, 63, 69–70, 84
    Progressive support, 53, 56–57
    railroads and, 27
    Red Scare and, 87–88
    skilled craftsmen, 51–53
    Franklin Roosevelt and, 90
    Theodore Roosevelt and, 69–70

welfare capitalism and, 72
World War I and, 86–87
See also strikes
United Mine Workers of America
(UMWA), 6, 53–54, 63, 69–70
U.S. Steel Corporation, 59, 72
United States v. E.C. Knight Company, 25

V
Vanderbilt family, 19–20
voting rights, 10, 35, 38, 40–42, 58, 82,
90

W
Wald, Lillian, 40
Walling, William English, 46
wealthy class
attitudes of, 18–20
envy of, 71
living conditions, 18–20
social Darwinism and, 15–16
Weaver, James, 22
welfare capitalism, 72
Wharton, Edith, 70
White, William Allen, 24, 40

Willebrandt, Mabel Walker, 45
Wilson, Woodrow
changing attitude toward Progressives, 75–76, 78, 82
influence on, 88
League of Nations, 75, 89
prohibition of alcohol, 44
Red Scare and, 88
woman suffrage, 41–42
World War I and, 75, 80, 82–83
Wobblies, 54, 56, 84
women
as activists for women's rights, 37,
40–41
as guardians of morality and families,
37
at Ludlow Massacre, 62
1920 election and, 89–90
in settlement house movement, 37–39
in temperance movement, 37, 43
as workers, 48–49, 54, 57, 59
Women's Christian Temperance Union
(WCTU), 37, 43
Women's Trade Union League, 37, 57

Picture Credits

Cover, pp. 4–5, 33, 39, 45, 60, 89 Bettmann/Contributor/Bettmann/Getty Images; pp. 6 (top), 50, 56, 65, 69 Everett Historical/Shutterstock.com; p. 6 (bottom left) Niday Picture Library/Alamy Stock Photo; p. 6 (bottom right) Everett Collection Inc/Alamy Stock Photo; pp. 7 (top left), 9, 10, 22, 28, 35, 55, 67, 74, 81, 85 Courtesy of the Library of Congress; p. 7 (top right) Hulton Archive/Stringer/Hulton Archive/Getty Images; pp. 7 (bottom), 14 Buyenlarge/Contributor/Archive Photos/Getty Images; p. 15 Edward Gooch/Stringer/Hulton Archive/Getty Images; p. 17 George Rinhart/Contributor/Corbis Historical/Getty Images; p. 18 FPG/Staff/Archive Photos/Getty Images; p. 19 Fotoluminate LCC/Shutterstock.com; pp. 26, 62 Fotosearch/Stringer/Archive Photos/Getty Images; p. 31 Collection of the New-York Historical Society, USA/Bridgeman Images; p. 34 Stock Montage/Contributor/Archive Photos/Getty Images; p. 41 Library of Congress/Contributor/Corbis Historical/Getty Images; p. 52 Wirtz Library/Wikimedia Commons; p. 73 Caesura/Wikimedia Commons; p. 79 Topical Press Agency/Stringer/Hulton Royals Collection/Getty Images; p. 86 Keystone/Stringer/Hulton Archive/Getty Images.

About the Author

David Anthony is the author of several nonfiction books for children and young adults, and he is also an elementary school teacher. David graduated from college with his master's degree in elementary education, and he has a passion for teaching his students to read and encouraging them to love books as much as he does. In his spare time, David enjoys spending time with his family, watching nature documentaries, and traveling.